BURNING
WORLDS

The First Principle of Creation

Suzanne Drexel Franzen

My deepest gratitude to CG Arron for the insistence on correctness. She is responsible for the preparation of this book for publication, and for the original cover picture is from her brother Paul.

ISBN: 1519163266
ISBN 13: 9781519163264
Library of Congress Control Number: 2015918787
CreateSpace Independent Publishing Platform
North Charleston, South Carolina

DEDICATION

for **Drexel Sanford Oliva**

at 80 years old, she announced what I too have learned:
Life is short, I do not know anything, and anything is possible.

At 90 years old she said:
My theory is that everything that ever was or ever will be is
happening right now. That means we can go back in history
and find out what really happened.

She is and always will be my mother.

TABLE OF CONTENTS

INTRODUCTION

The source of this book is not of this world. I have no claim to the information as its author. What you are about to read came through ten Quantum Healing Hypnosis Therapy sessions with a single client. Developed by the late Dolores Cannon, QHHT is a regression and progression hypnotic process giving a client access to his or her own subconscious.

The client contacted me through my website, http://QHHT-kauai.com. He told me that he was 59 years old and "dying from the inside out." Scheduled for cancer chemotherapy and surgery before the end of that year, he asked for a session to help him understand what was happening to him and why. His anger and frustration were holding him in bondage, so he could only fight his disease with no relief.

When Grapo came to his first appointment, I immediately felt a connection with him from previous lifetimes. He was and is my beloved brother. I welcomed him with a big hug. Being with him again felt like the most natural thing in the world. What he got out of the first session and the subsequent sessions has stayed with me, deeply affecting me ever since.

Normally, QHHT sessions access early life experiences, past life experiences or future life experiences. This client was different. His sessions merged his personality self with his subconscious self or higher self, who has direct connection with Guides, Ascended Masters, and other beings of Light, which together we call "the Guidance."

The information Grapo brought through in the first session concerned his own transition. He communicated important new information about the structure or process of aligning our many bodies at the end of physical life, and the help we get doing this. The old idea of death changed to the idea of transition.

In subsequent sessions, the Guidance came in and instructed us in a unique way. Each session began with a stage set, like in a theatrical play. As the scene opened, a Guide presented a block of information like a narrator. Topics covered include who we are, the structure of Creation, and what is beyond Creation. Guides taught us about the meaning of life here on Earth, how we can best perceive this meaning, interact with it and live it. Guides showed the progression of our many lives through Creation and back Home to All That Is. They explained "putting on the brakes" in the stream of energy that takes us Home. This fascinating journey is the grandest adventure we have. It is life.

Honoring my client's request for anonymity, the man transmitting this information here is called "Grapo," a name given to him by one of his Guides, named here as "Sister." She showed up in these sessions to share the story of Creation, Transition and Going Home. Other Guides joined us for other sessions, in this journey of expanded awareness and reality perception.

The messages are presented here as they came to us, edited very lightly for clarity and style, but never for content. Some thoughts and explanations are added where appropriate for greater understanding and flow of the transmitted material. I have used the format that Dolores Cannon uses in her books to indicate whom is speaking.

S = Suzanne (me), QHHT practitioner and session facilitator.

GR= Grapo, the receiver of the messages from his higher self and the Guides.

GHS: = A merged, Theta brain wave state of awareness with Grapo, his higher self and the Guides.

G = A guide or guides.

The description of Grapo's first QHHT session includes part of the hypnotic induction script taught by Dolores Cannon. (see http://www.dolorescannon.com) As a practitioner, I use Dolores's induction script as she taught it because the script efficiently guides clients into a theta state of relaxation, the space where the connection to the higher self exists. The same induction script was used to begin every session.

Grapo goes easily into the theta state, and the Guides come in with a *stage set* or *scene* that serves as a metaphor for the lesson to be delivered. Grapo is in direct conversation with Guidance. He and I both ask questions to get clarification as we go along.

Grapo is grappling with first-hand experiences of something extraordinary and quite outside of ordinary experience. His vivid sensations in the sessions are more real to him than his everyday life. He is trying to convey meanings through words that do not begin to match his session experiences. This is both frustrating and profound for him. When he speaks about his experiences to us, who lack a similar experience, the power of his perception can be lost. An analogy might be that he is trying to tell us about being swept away by a giant ocean wave when we have never seen an ocean nor even imagined one. We have no frame of reference to understand the ideas of an ocean or a wave.

Still, we are trying to convey to you a new perspective of life here on Earth that Grapo has shared from his Guides. We are delving to areas of consciousness here that we humans are beginning to explore and share more openly. We are pointing in the direction of something brand new. Few of us have experienced anything close to this view of *reality*.

We hope you will read this book as if you are listening to the sessions yourself in real time. Imagine what all the messages mean to you, as we have been imagining. The Guidance has been gracious in offering this to us now, as we get ready for our next steps in evolution. Having this information may make the journey more meaningful and precious to you. Humanity is evolving. The butterfly is emerging from its cocoon.

Enjoy the journey.

A MESSAGE FROM THE GUIDES: NEW WORLDS

We hope these messages bring some level of clarity to you, to all of humanity when they wish to see what is next.

Humanity has already been given the gift of the path of the Burning Worlds that do not burn souls. [see Chapter 7]

Each path takes you to the next Burning World. What comes next is what is given to you as a gift by the living God in this physical world, in this physical universe.

He awaits us anew in the new world which burns with the light that does not burn souls. That is what humanity yearns for. This is their new home.

It's the gift of the Christ Consciousness - for you to know and understand this clarity. You must understand it, not only on the level of consciousness and on the level of Being but also on the level of compassion, on the level of your heart. If you envision the living Christ with his hands down and open, this is his gift to you. This is the context of your new understanding. This is why we expressed the First Principle. All is flowing, non-stopping in the stream of life in the physical world. All is flowing from one Burning World that does not burn souls, into the next Burning

World that does not burn souls. The element of fire is the living love of God's consciousness in this world.

This consciousness is what our beloved Earth desires and flows towards. This is what humanity flows towards. There is no stopping the flow. No one can stop it, not other Beings, not other wills.

This awareness is the gift we give to you, that which expresses the First Principle, embodying and expressing the will of the Living Light and the Source of All that Is and Is Not. And yes, there is more for humanity at the end of the journey through the Burning Worlds, at the end where we meet and return to our shared Source. This comes at the end of the network of the Burning Worlds that do not burn souls. This is your journey. This is mankind's journey, one world at a time. Whatever level of consciousness you travel, it is still one world at a time. We are here to see that you travel. We will help you every day in every way and in every effort. It cannot be stopped.

We are Guides. We come to you to bring clarity and understanding not only on the level of consciousness, but also on the level of the heart, so that intellects can more fully understand and experience more deeply what is happening as you evolve on your journeys.

We bring you Peace and the love of the everlasting Source through the Burning Worlds that do not burn souls.

Be At Peace.

CHAPTER 1
INNER BODIES AND OUTER BODIES

*G*rapo *provides us with new information on the assistance we get when it's time for us to transition out of this body.*

What happens after we drop the body has been written about in many places. You can find this information in the ample literature on Near Death Experiences. Every religion (and science too) addresses this. The metaphysicians are way ahead in describing a bigger reality than the one we learned in school or church. The field of hypnosis opens the door for anyone who wants to experience their past lives, future lives, parallel lives, and more.

What has not been written about yet, is that on some level, we know when our time has come, or is about to come. That is when we start getting more direct help. You do not have to wait to die before you get to know what is next.

Grapo surprised me when he came up with this information. His contact with the area of consciousness that is not usually available to our minds, in our limited reality as humans, was immediate and profound. He did not miss a step as he leapt into this unexplored area in his Quantum Healing Hypnosis Therapy (QHHT) session.

1

During our lives, we receive assistance to sustain functioning at the highest level personally possible. This is different for each individual, as we each come into this life with a soul plan that includes "illness", "disease" or "success' in order to have those specific types of living and dying or transitional experiences. Usually, there is an explanation available, and it can be found through hypnosis. There are several avenues for evaluating the information gained from regression therapy, which will not be addressed here, for Grapo showed me something new. He surprised me when he came up with this experience.

Session 1: The Monitor

Grapo's breath deepens as he relaxes into the theta state.

He first stops at what he imagines is the most beautiful place in the world. For him, it seems a fantasy place. He sees a meadow with grayish green grass. The sky is pinkish red. He feels a slight breeze. Most astonishing, though, are the balloon characters floating around the mountains. They seem to him like cartoons.

From there, floating on a cloud, he arrives at a place with both mountains and a dessert. Huge, cube-like buildings float above the mountains. Grapo describes one cube as a library. He is floating outside this building.

Grapo has a physical body in this space. He is tall, thin, and cylindrical. He is wearing a gold and black garment that shimmers.

It's dark inside, but there is light coming through the windows. Inside is a mixture of arches, dark wood and books. The place feels mechanical to him. He asks and is told that the function of this place is to serve as a repository for stores of knowledge. It's a place to go and do research.

He asks how to get the information. They show him rather than tell him. He moves to a room where there is a Monitor.

GR: I am standing on the rim of a pool of water. Someone else is here directing me, the Monitor. He is tall and slender. He has a beard. He knows what is going on here. I am standing on the rim of this circular pool. It is not water although it's a kind of liquid. I am looking into it. I see another person here. He is manipulating some kind of machine, but there does not seem to be anything happening.

The pool now changes into a bright green liquid with light coming out. It smashes into my forehead and goes down my spine. I am glowing with this dark green light, radiating a green aura. I am standing there.

S: What is the purpose of this light?

GR: He says it's cleansing the memory and the body at the same time.

Now I am standing in the middle of the pool. The green light is going around me in waves. It's flowing around and around me.

S: What is going on here?

GR: I am asking the Monitor, and he says I am being worked on. My inner bodies are misaligned, they lack coordination. He says I have come out of time, not in this time, not of this place. It's another world.

S: To get this essence input we have to go to another place. Is that right?

GR: I am asking. The Monitor says this is the place people come to re-align and re-establish inner equilibrium. Beings come here to heal from all over the galaxy. What is happening for me has something to do with other bodies. It seems like we are bodies within bodies.

Here the Monitor speaks more directly with us. (M=Monitor) The higher self also participates in the conversation (GHS:).

M: The outer body is not in alignment with the physical body. If it's not in alignment, there is a disruption in the physical body. This process is helping to stabilize all the bodies within bodies. The effects are only temporary.

S: As these bodies come into alignment will there be some relief of Grapo's physical condition?

GHS: The effects are only temporary. The inner bodies are changing too fast. It's like dolls within dolls, like Russian dolls.

The inner ones are changing. The outer one cannot make the change. If we shed one body, there is no loss. There is always wholeness. It's like shedding skin. Each body holds a place and a time. Another body holds a different time and place. There is a loss of concern for the old body. It does not become necessary any longer. This is a part of the process. It's necessary and natural.

S: And we do it over and over again?

GHS: Yes. As we move from place to place the body creates its own harmony.

M: We are allowing the green light to continue its work on all the bodies to bring them into alignment and integrity.

S: While this continues, I would like to ask a few questions. Grapo has some concerns he would like answered. May I speak to his subconscious now?

GHS: Yes

S: Grapo wants to know, "What is going on?"

GHS: He is in transition. It's not a question of deciding. The process is continuous. He needs to roll with it. The physical breakdown is okay. He knows he came here [to earth] as an observer. He is done with that work. He can play now. He cannot control the events in this world. His work is in the silence now. He is out of time. He will remain in the body only a short time now.

S: He would like for this experience of transitioning to be easy, graceful even pleasant.

GHS: The diseases he is experiencing are caused by the transition of the other bodies. The physical body is being disrupted by the changes in the other bodies. His physical body cannot make this transition. The essence of the Being is being aligned. This body may not heal. Disease is not necessary for transition. A transition can be made with a well body, too.

S: Grapo has expressed to me that he has a lot of frustration and anger. Is it part of the process? He wants to know if having diseases is a lesson or a way to get off the planet?

GHS: Neither. There is responsibility in both places. The bodies are not ready, so it's difficult to distinguish between which is responsibility and which is play. He can play in both places.

Grapo is experiencing upset at this time. We do some further smoothing and relaxing before continuing.

S: Does transitioning mean that the body cannot stay on earth?

GHS: No, it cannot.

S: Why are you giving him this experience?

GHS: To give him assurance. A greater perception of wholeness. His task is a continuance. There is joy in transitioning!

S: Would it be appropriate for him to know where he comes from?

GHS: He is part of the Source. He knows that. He has had many lifetimes on earth.

S: Will he be coming back here?

GHS: That cannot be answered from this place. He is free to go, it's his choice. The process in this world is a goal of continuance. To heal is not the focus.

S: He wants to know if he should stay in the medical system?

GHS: It is part of this world. It will manifest the results that will help in his transition. There will be a lessening of the frustration and anger, as he understands this.

Each moment of this life is a final gift. Be present to receive this gift. Know you are never alone. It is part of the process of letting go of attachments to this world. Let go of worries. The focus is change. Play now. We are working on assisting him to make the transition. It is a process of letting go of attachments. You will be letting go of your attachment to your body, the earth, life, things, people, family, everything of this reality. Everyone does this.

S: If doubt comes up, what can he do?

GHS: We are of the Light. We are most accessible when he is in silence. We are always present. He needs to be aware of our presence. He can visualize the green pool and remember that he is being assisted. He is part of *us.* We meet him in the silence. This is part of the process of letting go of the attachment to this world. Play and let attachments go. Let go of your concerns of what may or may not be. The focus is change. Be At Peace.

Debrief of First Session

The debrief for this session comes a week later. There is much discussion as new ideas emerge. Grapo says more about what was going on for him, experiences that were not voiced during the session.

G: One of the biggest questions I had was whether this was going to be my own imagination, or if I would control the images. I wanted to find out for myself. I did. As I got relaxed and started visualizing, I realized that although I was consciously aware of being hypnotized, the smaller self was *not* going to control it because this was being guided from somewhere else.

The other thing I want to say is that I never suspected that I was going to be involved in spreading knowledge. I knew I had come into many lifetimes as an observer, and to find out that I am now going to be bringing in information that has not been here before is exciting.

I knew that I was supposed to report what was happening in the session, so it would be on the recording, but that was hard to do. There was so much energy coming through that it was overwhelming. There were a couple of times I teared up. I was not sad. I never at one moment felt sad. The whole process was bliss because the energy overwhelmed me physically. It was so intense, and the body had to react to it. That is why there are all those periods of silence. It's a good thing you asked me questions, or else I would not have been able to say anything.

There was something else I wanted to tell you about. When I moved to another world, everything was a reflection of dark green. It was almost like dusk, and I was literally floating above the grass. The grass was tall and the blades were dark, dark green. The scene was quite subdued. The impression I got was one of total calmness, real peace. I was basically floating above the grass. I thought, "Wow, this world is really green," but there were some differences. I think I pointed out earlier that there were trees and rolling hills. You instructed me as to how calming it was to be there and how relaxed I was. It was almost like a healing then.

The thing was that the trees were huge and the leaves were the color of cherry blossoms, a beautiful white pinkish color. I thought that was kind of odd. Instead of a bluish background behind the clouds, in this world, it was a magenta sky. Then, there were the creatures above the clouds. They were like magicians working with balloons, and they would twist the balloons, so they had funny shapes. They were transparent, so I could see through them. I got the impression they were intelligent. They were gliding over the trees very softly. I wanted to go to them, but you asked me to float on the cloud and go someplace else.

When I got to the next *place,* the first impression I had was that I was in the middle of the Sahara Desert. Lots of bright sand, and then I saw what I thought were mountains, but they were buildings.

They were all right angles, six stories tall with only one opening, like a door. They had no other features, but these cubes were very fascinating to see. When I went into one through a portal, it was cool inside. Some places were like a Victorian library, with stacks. In other places, it was more modern. It was light but not lit by lamps or anything I could see. Of course, I was so fascinated. I wanted to go into this room and that room.

I walked down a hall and got into this one room where I met the Monitor. I had the first impression that he and I were the same, but not really. He was tall, about 7 feet tall with a humanoid face, a beard and sideburns, and a pointed mustache.

He was very intelligent, and when I communicated with him, I got the impression right off the bat that this is someone who radiated intelligence and patience. I mainly was thinking about what he was saying to me.

He was wearing a robe kind of outfit, and I thought it was scaly, but it was not. It was black and gold and the patterns of his clothing were paisley. It was regal and florescent and shiny.

He was very gentle. He did not make any sudden moves to scare me. He gave me the impression that he was physically very calm - kind of like a doctor.

Way down the room, which seemed semi-alive, there was an oval shape on the floor. He basically told me to go stand by the shape. I kept thinking, "What is this?" At one point it looked like a pattern on the floor, a white pattern. He said, "Yes, it is white." Then it started to change into a light bubbly shimmering substance. It was bright fluorescent with so many shades of green it was almost hypnotic. While I was trying to figure this out, he was at a small table with an instrument panel, and he was manipulating the panel.

The next thing I knew there was a light, like a 2x4 beam of light that came out of the pool. It struck me in the forehead and went through the back of my head about three or four feet. I froze. I could not move for some reason. I stood there, and I was thinking the whole time, "This is really fascinating." I asked him what he was doing. He looked at me and said, "Well, throughout the whole Galaxy, people come here for this healing." I said, "Well, I know I have a physical ailment, and that is what the healing is for." He looked at me, kind of puzzled and said, "No, this is not about the cancer."

That was not what I wanted to hear.

I stood there and looked again at the pool. All of a sudden, I was in the middle of the pool. I was not looking at my physical body anymore. I was looking at a humanoid body, but I could not see any physical details. I was looking through the body. Inside were these wavelike patterns forming out of the green energy. I consciously made an effort to find out if I could see what I looked like. An answer came back saying, "No, absolutely not. Stay there and experience what is going on."

So I asked, "What is going on? What is this?"

He said, "It's your inner bodies. That is what we are working on as opposed to what you see as your cancer issue." I got the distinct impression he was saying that the cancer issue was irrelevant and not to focus on that. "Our focus and purpose here is your inner bodies," he said. He gave me the explanation that the inner bodies are like those Russian dolls nestled inside each other. They were working on the inner bodies for the transition.

The transition was from another time and space, another level of consciousness. It was like being in two places at once while realizing that this physical body and another body were being energized or prepared, somehow. They were preparing for a light body. The physical body could not handle the energies that were coming through the light body. There was corruption; that is what they see as the cancer. I was kind of torn. Why would you prepare my inner body and let the other body go while I am still living in it? That is when they told me that life is not like that. It's not being in a place only once. It's a question of perception. Life is a continuous stream, constantly existing simultaneously. Because of this world, we have a perception of beginning and ending, but they say the continuous stream from their perspective has no beginning and no end.

It was my misunderstanding that I was suffering. I was not suffering the degradation of this body. In fact, they were more than fine that the whole process was preparing me for transition to another life. That means I cannot see it as, "Why am I suffering in this earth? Why does God allow this to happen?"

That question does not apply, I was told. It's a free choice world. We always have free choice on this continuum. That is why, when you asked if I would be coming back as human, they were not able to answer.

For them, a choice is made in the moment, and can be changed. I was told that I had not made that choice yet, but they were preparing me so that when I did decide, the bodies would be ready.

That was when I felt my physical hypnotized body sinking into the sofa. I was so heavy, and at the same time I was getting lighter and lighter. It was a huge contrast, and it was a wonderful experience because that was the freedom I can taste. I can enjoy it. I wish the session did not end then, for I have so many other questions, but I got the answer I was really seeking: Do not worry about the cancer as a kind of punishment for something. It also is not a lesson I have to learn, either. That was a big relief, to know this is a process concerning the energies of what this body can handle. There is no concept of punishment or cruelty or anything like that.

One moment to the other, after being in the body, there comes no beginning or no end, a smooth simple straight through, a non-event into another existence. That is why they were kind of puzzled by my concern about the disease process. It's all part of the process of being here. Here you can break a leg, or be in an accident, and think you are suffering, but in the absolute reality, in the light body, they do not see suffering at all. They know we suffer, but they see a bigger picture. They are not as stressed out as we are here.

They say this is time to *not* attach to all of those feelings and energies because you are transitioning. This is not even a question to get asked. It's part of the process you are going through. I felt a lot of my concerns float away, disappear, because I know now that where I am going is amazing. It's part of the continuum.

They gave me the concept to play and enjoy myself in this world.

What matters is not in this world. What matters is where ever you are in your lifestream. There is no loss whatever happens. There is no need to hang onto those things we find so precious. It's a continuum. We need to detach to all of it for the transition to be made smoothly.

You can come to your own conclusions about the material shared through and from Grapo. I now will offer what has been revealed to me since his first session.

I know now that it's possible to be comforted consciously by our higher self as we progress through the experience of leaving the body. There is never any loss. They said that! It is very similar to walking out of a movie and then going into another one. What we have not realized before is that we can have contact with the experiences of the transition from another place, outside of the commonly agreed upon reality of our daily lives.

One thing I noticed was that the place Grapo visited to have his bodies aligned was available for anyone, if that was what they needed. The Monitor at the pool seemed to be doing his job as though it was easy, as though he did this all day everyday. Later, when we asked about this we were told that this is not limited to the humans on earth. This place is available to the Universe. We did not hear how far this extended.

The Monitor's form was a form that would be comfortable for Grapo, and was in a way a reflection of him. I surmise from this that whoever comes for an alignment of bodies will "see" a Monitor who is comfortable for them to see.

What intrigues me now is this: We were told that there is more to be revealed, and this is the beginning of an expansion of awareness. We are more than we ever thought we could be and more is going on than we have ever seen before. It's to be revealed now.

We are ready.

CHAPTER 2
THE FIRST PRINCIPLE OF CREATION

*W*e sit together talking, wondering what will come out of the second *session. Many awarenesses came through for both of us during the week before the session. Our beginning talk was lively. We came up with a couple of things we wanted to know more about. We got more than we bargained for. Here is our conversation, followed by the session itself.*

Beginning Conversation
GR: We are not denied aware consciousness. It's our option and our perception that makes us use lower unaware consciousness rather than higher aware consciousness. That is why we see things as duality, as separate from everything else -- us, them, other places.

One of my big questions is, why do we forget? I am beginning to wonder if forgetting is not a function of memory, but a function of what level of consciousness we are on. I do not know who said it, maybe I read it somewhere or heard it on television, that we only use around 15 watts of power in our brain. That is not very much energy. So, maybe we cannot remember because we do not have enough wattage. I'm not sure, but it comes into play.

We have this idea of why we are here. We get a lot of those experiences and understandings from other people. Is this our training ground? Is this a lesson plan? That is my big question. If Source sent one billion people to earth to experience earth life, what is the difference if I go? Are not one billion minds equivalent to one billion super computers on some level? Shouldn't they be able to experience the totality of what the earth is like without me being here? So, why is there a concept of classes and learning and drama going on? It seems like there must be something more coherent, more simple than that. After we did the first session, when I was talking to Daren (his friend) explaining what was going on, I had the distinct feeling that there was something more, something else they did not tell me.

S: Right.

GR: Then you came back and said the same thing. There was something else to be revealed. I have an intuitive feeling that maybe there is not as much drama going on as people think. I do not know what it is or how to explain it. It's kind of frustrating because all I see is the drama. I can experience higher consciousness without the drama, but I cannot see the connection. That is what I am curious about. What is the connection? What is the process going on here? That is why I was asking you what Dolores Cannon was doing; (*this conversation having happened before Dolores Cannon's death in 2014*) if she was getting an impression that there was more going on than ETs running around trying to help us. Apparently, from what I read and what I see, some people think there is some kind of war going on, but I do not see ETs, and I do not see the war.

S: Yeah.

GR: I have not run into a reptilian yet.

S: Unless they are disguised?

GR: Yeah. I take it with a grain of salt because I do not have that experience. I do not know. Maybe it's because my perspective is more towards consciousness, rather than that level of physical reality... but, I am curious.

S: I am curious, too. I guess that is why we are doing these sessions.

GR: I'd be the first one to be dumbfounded if higher consciousness says that I am an ET, or I am descended from some reptilian.

S: Maybe we all are. Last night I had a profound dream. You and I were in a meeting with some very aware beings. One woman all in white was giving us information. I was leaning up against you. I felt we were both being given this information. These other beings were there, and they gave us a bunch of information, too. I saw pages, and I saw diagrams for a book. Of course, I cannot remember them now.

They wanted us to know this book is going to be good. They were encouraging us and saying to keep going with this, even if it seems slow at times, or you get impatient, keep going because it's going to be good. The whole idea was that we have only tapped into the start of this process. We do not really have the whole story yet.

GR: To change the subject, there is one thing I am curious about, if you can ask about it. I saw something on YouTube about free energy. I am curious because I always thought about going into electronics, but I didn't think I had the mindset to do electronics. I did not get this concept of electricity flowing. Anyway, I flipped on this one YouTube video where this guy was saying, "Here it is. This is free energy," I watched it three times, but it did not make any sense. I read the comments, and everybody was saying the same thing, so I did not feel so stupid. Then somebody said, "Oh, I get it, the rocks."

The guy in the video took a steel bowl, and he had a little round tube of steel or some kind of metal. He put the tube in a bowl, and then he put these rocks around the tube in the bowl. He attached one wire to the edge of the steel bowl, and he attached another wire to the tube in the middle of the rocks inside the bowl. Then he hooked up one of those heavy-duty twelve-inch pulley motors. He put one wire on each side of the motor, and the motor ran. I thought, where's that electricity coming from? It seemed to go through the wires to the motor but it was hooked up to a bowl full of rocks.

S: Rocks!

GR: Yeah. And the comment was that the rocks were radioactive.

S: Oh.

GR: I guess they are not radioactive to the point where they are dangerous, only slightly radioactive. He calls them Japanese rocks, probably because he got them from Japan somewhere near Fukushima. But it still didn't make any sense. Why would radiation, which is all over the place, be in these little rocks? He had about 20 little rocks piled around the core tube. Why would it cause electricity to run? It does not make any sense at all.

But he was saying it does work. It's dumbfounding because other people create a similar set of tools with a special tube, so they can look really cool. They charge you $50 to a couple thousand dollars for this type of thing to put a light bulb on it. He says all the tools he has there cost him 50 cents.

So, I have always wondered about technology because if this world is going to get enlightened, it has to get off fossil fuel and get over the consumption of everything. Energy needs to be free. People need to be free. I am not talking about people who spend 20 years or 15 years meditating. I am talking about the average individual that rarely turns inward. They need a means to get them free from whatever is enslaving their lives. There must be some way of creating devices that free people from the capitalist way. It's a form of slavery, in my mind, because it takes you away from your responsibility for yourself.

S: Absolutely.

GR: The focus is on things rather than on people. That is why primitive societies tend to be more healthy than we are. They deal with what they need, and they deal with nature while standing right next to it. We are so separated from all that. Part of it is because of the way we created our society, not just in America, but in the rest of the world, too. We pull ourselves away from doing the work we need to do, and instead we spend our time doing work other people need us to do to get done the things they want done.

S: I noticed a long time ago that there is something wrong with the system. Take the American dream of owning your own home. Most people work their butts off to pay for the home, so they are never home. They are out doing the work to earn the money to support the house that they are not home to enjoy.

GR: And when they get home, they are dead tired. Their relationship with each other goes to pot, and they are yelling at each other. The American Dream tells you to have all those lovely kids that you want to get away from.

S: It's ridiculous. Anyway, free energy; we want to know more about free energy. It would be interesting to see what they will let us know about that, too.

GR: Yeah, I think we lost a lot of ground when we lost Tesla. He was a genius.

S: We went a different direction. We took a different path.

GR: I think we didn't get a choice because other people decided for us, because they could not make enough money with Tesla's ideas.

S: You see, that was the choice: " We have to make money. "

We started with the usual hypnosis induction. When he got to the most beautiful place in the world, I had him go into a deeper state of theta brain waves than ever before. He instantly moved to a scene with a big pyramid.

Session 2: Consciousness Always Moves Forward

S: When you are ready, you can give some description of what is happening, what you see, what you feel, what you smell, what you know or sense.

GHS: There is a big pyramid, and a big rectangle building seems to be on the roof. It seems to be a reflection of the pyramid and the sky. Looks like Egypt of some kind, but it's not Egypt. It is not in this world. It is a reflection. There seems to be a podium of some kind, and a light pyramid is in the sky. There is another person there. Seems to be another one of the Monitors. I get the impression he's communicating with other like sites.

S: With other like sites? Is that what you said?

GHS: Yeah. This is one structure of many. It's some kind of communication center, but it's outside on the balcony, on one of the pyramids. The outside of the pyramid looks like it's coated in some kind of shell or enamel or something. I cannot seem to get a clear picture of the operator.

S: I'd like you to ask if this is another lifetime, that Grapo is engaged in, and if it's appropriate to explore it as a lifetime.

GHS: No. I am a visitor here.

S: Okay. It's good to be clear about that. So, why have you come to this place?

GHS: So I can communicate with other places. From here I can be transported from place to place. It's like a communication portal. They can open the portal, so you can travel.

S: Have you come there just to know that, or are you going to travel?

GHS: I feel some resistance in being here. It seems to me it's technology. I do not feel the energy. It's almost like a way station, so you can travel from place to place.

S: Who decides where you are going to travel?

GHS: You decide. It's kind of like a bus terminal.

S: So, you have come here because you decided that you are going to travel somewhere. How do you know where you are going?

GHS: I do not know.

S: Is there someone you can ask? You said there was somebody like the Monitor. Can you call in somebody that knows. That is always the easy way, to let you know where you are going to go. And, when you are ready you can do that, and you can go.

GHS: I walked through a portal. I seem to be in a strange kind of city with a series of white walls. There seems to be an escalator of some type that goes up to a large, round terrace. I do not see or have a sense of a base or a ground anywhere. It's kind of floating. There are people on the terrace. They are talking, relaxing, like it's an everyday activity, like in a normal city. People are talking to one another. It's almost like a busy cafe.

S: Do you hear voices, or is it more a telepathic communication in some way?

GHS: I cannot hear them talking, but I can hear them. Seems like they are talking about everyday activities in their lives. I do not know if there is a purpose to this place.

S: Did the Monitor come with you, or are you on your own now?

GHS: I am on my own.

S: Okay. But you chose to come here to this platform.

GHS: Yes, another Monitor points to a doorway. I see the city, and I walk through to it.

S: What we know so far is that you chose to come to this place, that there is a reason for you to come here. If the reason is not right there on the platform, it may be a little ahead in the story. Let's move forward in time to a day that has an important event happening. You can do that now. So what is it that is happening?

GHS: I have moved to what looks like a hallway with a large room, like a room with tables. There is someone sitting there. I cannot see them very clearly. I am asking why I am here. I'm told that I am here because I need answers. I am confused because the energy here feels very normal. It does not feel like there is much depth.

S: Are the answers available in this place? In this room you are in?

GHS: It depends on what I am asking.

S: Where do the answers come from?

GHS: There is someone here who can tell me the answers.

S: Okay. Let's ask the questions that you want to ask. If we do not get answers, we'll go to a new place. What is it you want to ask? You can go ahead and ask.

GHS: I am asking about the technology, the use of energy. They said it coincides with the changes on the earth right now. We are becoming aware of what is possible. I am seeing the experiment. I am asking how the radioactive rocks move electricity. They say it's not the radiation that is moving the electricity. They say it's actually consciousness moving, creating a process. The materials are tools they use. It's a much subtler form of action going on. They say consciousness is flowing, and the electricity flows with it because we desire it.

This is the connection between the new and the old world. In the old world we created principles, calculations and structures. In the new world, we use consciousness. Consciousness flows, structure is created, and energy moves. It's one world superimposed on another. You can play with the physical properties like the bowls, rocks and wires. As consciousness evolves, the energies allow it to function differently. We cannot use our intellectual principles to understand. It just looks like it's functioning on a physical level. They could use a tool to focus on what we desire, but it's consciousness that creates it.

S: So, what is it going to take for us to be able to activate this energy and use it? What is going to transpire for us to be able to do that?

GHS: There was a time in your world where you had magic. Magic, as described as mana. When creation first came to life, all the physical sciences came to life. As the universe expanded, the physical principles changed. The expansion cannot happen without changing the physical properties of this universe. Those energies that you used to make magic were only existent for a very short time in this world, but it profoundly affected the thinking of mankind. As the universe expanded, the physical properties of those energies changed. The physical laws do not remain the same. You lost contact with those energies of magic. They are still there, but they are not within your reach. For a brief moment in man's history, within a briefly held understanding, one could touch that energy. But as the universe expanded, the principles of understanding changed, and mankind could not keep up.

So, the new technologies are an expression of that time where the universe has expanded to a point that mankind can, through consciousness, create new technology. It will take some time for them to understand how these things work because they are still functioning on the old principles. The laws of physics have changed. Quantum possibilities are evolving. The intellect is slow to understand. The tools they are using now cannot grasp what is happening. Mankind must learn new tools, new ways of thinking.

S: Is mankind being assisted in that?

GHS: This is part and parcel of the physical evolution of this universe. Mankind flows in a stream along with the ever-expanding universe, ever expanding consciousness. Mankind's physical body is evolving, but the body is still trapped in the old understanding, and that is what is causing chaos. It's difficult for people to understand. People look for salvation, and they already have salvation. It's their evolution. It cannot be stopped.

The universe expands, the earth expands, consciousness and mankind expands. It's an immovable object, moving and changing. Play with the technology. Learn what you can do with it. The energy technology can only benefit you. Mankind is looking for guidance to understand the principles of these new energies. You do not have the means to understand, so it confuses you. Seeing is not believing in this case. But it will come.

S: Will some of these new technologies come into place, and then we will begin to discover and understand them, or will it be the other way around, that we understand and discover them, and then put them into place?

GHS: Humanity's conscious evolution must co-evolve along with the principles, the flow of consciousness. One cannot happen without the other. The universe is expanding, dragging mankind along. It's our choice to look at these new ways or remain with the old. The whole of the universe is changing. All species are evolving simultaneously. There is no consciousness without the expanding evolution of the physical universe. The physical universe will stop or end if it does not keep expanding. This is a necessary function of evolution, of evolving consciousness.

The drama is in the focus of each individual at this time. Individuals create their understanding either correctly or incorrectly. They can move with the expanding universe, or they stay where they are. They must decide. They must choose. It's like a speeding train that never stops, but you have a choice to get off. Mankind sees this change coming, but they are limited in their perspective. Each species focuses on their needs. Consciousness in the universe evolves despite their needs. It's their choice.

S: I do not know if this is an indicator or not, but I have been seeing a lot of things about animal communicators, being able to speak with animals. We are finding that animals have consciousness that is expanding, and we are able to speak with them, but not so much with words, but with pictures and with awareness. Is this part of the expansion happening?

GHS: Yes. Mankind is still not consciously aware to the point where they can understand what is going on as a whole. There are some who can, and they have singular pathways open to communicate. Mankind is becoming aware of intelligences beyond our own world. Even in our own world. It's not time for them to lie down with the lions, unless they want to be food.

S: I thought this food chain is part of what is changing, so animals will not be in the food chain with each other or with us. Is this promise part of the change in consciousness?

GHS: It will come, and you will not be with a human body. Flesh consumes flesh. This is the physical world. The world you desire is one without the bodies.

S: So, it's simply a condition of having a body that we have the food chain?

GHS: Yes. It's mostly a conscious choice to step out of the speeding evolution, to slow down, and to be in this place. This train, this flow, is always moving. It's your choice to get on or get off. It is not a punishment. It is not a reward. It is part of the process of evolution, both physical and in consciousness.

There are many worlds, many places you can go. The place you seek is beyond all physical reality. That is the Living Light. That is what draws consciousness. That is what draws the physical reality. Touch it, and do not resist it. We all flow in that direction. That place is without physical reality. It's the Living Light. Bring it into your awareness, and it will accelerate you ever closer to the One Source. That is the universal principle. The more you open your awareness to this flow of evolving consciousness, the faster you will move.

That is the First Principle. If you stop to play, you get off the flow. Actually, this flow never stops. You never stop, but you can slow down. You can play in this world or any other world. The choice is yours. But the First Principle is absolute, no matter how hard you slow down, no matter how hard you try to stop, no matter how much you enjoy the moment, you are always moving forward. That is the First Principle.

S: That is very beautiful, the way it's been designed. Grapo had a question about forgetting. Why is it that we came into this world, and we forgot all these things. What is the purpose of forgetting?

GHS: It's because we chose to stop and play in this world. When we stopped to play, we refocused ourselves to the consciousness of this level of this physical world. We did not forget. We chose not to remember.

S: Slight difference there.

GHS: It's a way of putting on the brakes. We are putting on the brakes of evolution, of expanding consciousness, so we can focus in the moment.

The Source of Living Light is ever eternal and present. It does not need to focus in one place. It's everywhere at once. It is the singularity. It's the totality of all combined into one. It does not need duality. It does not need to stop to see. It's only we who choose to stop to see. And in observing this world, we remove ourselves temporarily from the stream. We change our focus from a wide view to one of a pinpoint focus. From our duality viewpoint it looks like we are stoping the train, but from a wider view we never stop moving. Evolution calls us as a magnet calls a nail. It is irresistible and unstoppable. It is the First Principle.

S: A very powerful principle. So when we put on the brakes, when we get off the train and have a human experience, that is okay, is it not?

GHS: Yes.

S: It's actually rather magnificent in its own way; each life experience is unique and precious. So, there is another question Grapo wanted to know more about.

GHS: The many bodies.

S: Yes. Many bodies I want to know about that, too.

GHS: Many bodies are created, so you can slow down and experience this world, but they are temporary bodies, because the First Principle cannot be stopped. The body transforms temporarily.

The evolution of the other bodies allows you to move faster and faster. But even in this journey to the Source, there are many places to stop.

S: So who is it that decided to stop and have a lifetime as Grapo?

GHS: The concept of individualism exists within the time frame of this physical world. It's necessary to help focus, to help be in this place. Being creates an identity. We interact with others by creating our Beings into existence. The Buddhists understood that we must let go of this existence, of our individual being, to return to the Source. Enlightenment is returning to the Living Light.

S: So, is this journey of being Grapo almost complete now? Is he ready to rejoin the river in the movement and expansion of consciousness?

GHS: Yes.

S: And that is what we are calling his transition?

GHS: It is all transitions. Once you return to the stream of expanding consciousness, the individual reality ceases to exist. The individual created that existence in that moment, when he [Grapo] came into existence through being. All of that is unraveled. It's of memory, experiences. His awareness is outside of that consciousness, outside of that reality. Be at peace.

S: Yes. Be at peace with what is. So, for the purposes of my education, what Grapo is experiencing as the changes in his physical body, do they really have anything to do with this transition, or is it a separate issue?

GHS: It's part of the transition. We all are transitioning. Some more willingly than others. If you understand the First Principle, that the universe is always moving forward, if you open your consciousness to experiencing the First Principle, the process of this reality seems to be happening faster. It's a perspective of being in this world.

S: Is it possible for humans to make the transition without manifesting deterioration of the body?

GHS: That depends on the degree of integration, of consciousness and the physical body. There are some who are fully integrated, and the process is quick. The body dissolves instantly from our perspective.

Opening ones self to the First Principle helps to accelerate the process, helps to integrate consciousness.

S: Grapo has spent a great deal of this lifetime doing things like meditation to become more aware. Is this helping him to make this transition more easily?

GHS: It took a lifetime of meditation, but it only took one moment of awareness, and the process is complete. Awareness became whole, and the focus was turned away from this world, back to the First Principle, and all that he is in this reality, will dissolve, and he will continue on to the Source.

Be at peace.

S: Yes. Be at peace. Be at peace. All is well. Is it all right if I ask a few more questions?

GHS: Yes.

S: Thank you. I am very grateful to have this opportunity. I'd like to ask about the dream that I had last night, where Grapo and I were together with a small group and they were showing me the book and diagrams and pages, and saying that it would all come forward easily. Was that a true dream? Is it truth that I was being shown?

GHS: Yes.

S: And as Grapo makes this transition, will there be more opportunities for us to get together and explore further? It seems to me that there is more than one place that we can do that, because we are connected in consciousness. It won't necessarily take the physical to accomplish what we are trying to accomplish, to help other people know that all is well. And whatever they are experiencing is a consequence of their expansion in consciousness. Am I still on track here?

GHS: In this world, the First Principle is the first truth.

S: Integrating that First Principle will carry us through all of it, won't it?

GHS: Yes. Many are looking for the way back. The First Principle is the way back.

That is the story of your book.

S: Oh, okay. It's nice to have that start. The diagrams in the dream I was shown last night, is that something that will be included in the book?

GHS: What we showed you in a dream is only meant to encourage you.

S: It did. I felt a great deal of love during that dream, and a great deal of connection, a great deal of support. It was all very lovely.

GHS: Yes. The connection is there.

S: I'd like to ask something. Grapo came to me several weeks ago with a desire not to suffer over this transition. Has that been integrated now, so there is no necessity to suffer?

GHS: To a point.

S: To a point. Can it be taken further today?

GHS: We can work on it.

S: Is it a matter of his perspective?

GHS: The physical body is in this physical world, and it must follow the principles of this physical world. He is getting help from many sources. He does not desire to suffer. But it will not end completely until he leaves this physical world. That is the property of this world, this existence.

S: As he continues to let go of all of his attachments to this physical world, will the suffering decrease?

GHS: All suffering will end when he leaves this world.

S: Simply release this world, and the suffering is over?

GHS: Suffering is a part of this reality. It's part of the drive of this reality.

S: Oh, this is a very interesting place to stop the train and investigate. When we are done, we are done.

GHS: When we leave, we leave all this. We leave behind the principles of this existence. We leave behind the choices of this world.

S: So if it's appropriate, and if it would support Grapo, can you give him an indication of how much more he has to complete before he will step through that portal into a new reality. Is he very close?

GHS: Contact with the First Principle brings him closer and closer. It accelerates the process.

S: And is that accomplished through his desire?

GHS: Yes. It's his desire. No concept of when. Not at this time.

S: Okay. Your instructions were, be at peace. So, be at Peace. We thank you for all of your input today during our time together. Thank you so much. Now we call back all of the personality of Grapo into this body remembering everything that he's experienced today, integrating it easily and peacefully.

Debrief After Session

GR: I am wondering what is feeling wonderful here - when I was being back with Source. That was wonderful.

S: And to know that we are going there. That is so great. We do not have to *only* go there. We can *go* whenever we want, like we did today. Well, that was very interesting. I am glad we got to do that.

GR: Yes. Sometimes questions were hard to focus on because the perspective was from a higher level of consciousness. I tried to figure out why you were asking questions that would mean dissolving to nonexistence of this individual, and for yourself eventually. The image I got was in the beginning — a lot of sacred texts say "in the beginning" — that in the beginning there was light, because the light was necessary to create physical reality, to create the universe. And when it created, when what we call the Big Bang happened, there was a Big Bang on another level, and that was the expansion of consciousness.

As light expanded our world, consciousness expanded outward. It got more and more refined. Like the physical universe as it expands our world, it gets more and more refined. Those energies coming into our reality in this world are coming because of that expansion. As we go through this expansion, the physical principles, what we call physics, changes. So, the *one* in the beginning is not the same *one* at the end.

We like to think in concrete terms. We like to design the most simple principles to express it all. You can do that in one sense, but in absolute reality, you cannot. The ever-expanding physical universe eventually is going to its completion, and consciousness will expand where it needs to be.

What I want to say is that when the universe expands to the point it becomes one with the Source, the Living Light, this physical reality will no longer need to exist. There is no single principle you can write or theorem you can write to express this physical universe. It is constantly changing. When the consciousness which is expanding with the universe comes to completion, this physical universe will cease to exist.

A lot of people say that this is a lesson plan. Yes, and no. It's a lesson plan just from our perspective. It also is a lesson plan from a higher level of consciousness, from all those celestial beings whom we think exist partially in our world and partially in their own level of existence. We tend to divide up reality, absolute reality, but we cannot. We are talking at one moment about duality, which is constantly changing choices. Karma is not bad or good. It's constantly changing choices. Karma is a way of saying, we change our choices so much that we are putting on the brakes. We are slowing down our evolution.

That is not a bad thing. We can stop and focus in this world. When you stop constantly making changes as you evolve consciously, you stop making choices. The closer and closer you get to your Source, there is less desire for you to make changes. With less desire to be here, you will instantly start moving by refocusing your view onto that stream. The Living Light is the Source. The First Principle is the understanding that we cannot put on the brakes completely or let go of the brakes completely.

S: Okay.

GR: The lesson plan is in this world, and in the next reality closest to this world. People say you can rewrite your lesson plan. That is true. But you are rewriting it to be in this world. You are not rewriting it to be closer to the Source.

S: Right.

GR: That is just another way of putting on the brakes. You ask the question, "When?" The answer basically is when you stop deciding to make choices, and instead, decide to return to Being the First Principle. The First Principle is focused on accelerating your conscious evolution by whatever means possible.

The Buddhists understood this, as did the Vedic tradition. In the Vedas, their whole process was to understand from an absolute point of view why this reality exists. Why does the First Principle exist in this world? They understood that to let go of all these realities, we have to stop the process of doing those realities in this world. We have to get to a state where we are beyond choices. They called that *Samadhi*. The Bhagavad Gita says to establish the self and then perform right action. You will be outside of duality, so whatever action you do, is going to be *of* the First Principle.

When Buddha died, the last thing he was talking about was liberation. I am not exactly sure what were the last words he said, but it was something to the effect that, "I should have meditated more." He was talking to his disciples about suffering and letting go. He knew at that very moment of death that he was still in this reality. He was still bound to this reality through the principle of karma, for that principle of changing your mind. It wasn't until he finally let go physically that his point of focus changed and this earth bound reality ceased to exist for him.

All the questions we are asking are irrelevant at that point. We are in that stream of consciousness. We are accelerating faster and faster to the Source. From that perspective, all our commotion about what is going to happen next, about what the light means, about what the energies that are coming in mean for individuals, for our political system, for our economic system, really, all that commotion has very little meaning, if any. We write the lesson plans as we come into this reality. We make our choices. Outside of this reality, in the stream of the First Principle, a lesson plan does not need to exist and does not exist.

Now, imagine what it looks like. Imagine thousands and millions of individuals traveling through this stream of light. All of a sudden they coalesce into a ball, and they fall out of that stream of light into this reality. We are all doing it. We are like these little balls creating our realities. Whether it's here in this planet or some other planet or some other galaxy or some other universe, however you want to phrase it, we are coalescing out of that wholeness of consciousness into the singularity of this individual life. When you leave individual reality behind and return to the stream of expanding consciousness, the expanding universe, all this does not mean anything anymore.

S: Right

GR: You've got it in your memory. You've got your experiences, and then you go on. But you are traveling along like a train, and there is a giant magnet pulling that train. There are no stops along the way. You have to jump off. Jumping off is when you coalesce from that vast stream of light into something that is physical reality.

That is the choice you have. Karma is you accelerating that choice, yes or no, all the time, going back and forth, which puts on the brakes. And so when you ask, "When is it time to leave?" they will always say, "You can leave any time you want. It's your choice."

From that perspective, a lot of the questions do not need to be asked. The real important information that came through was understanding that you can leave that process when you leave this world. You can coalesce out of this world and return to that expanding stream whenever you want. It's your choice.

There are a lot of beliefs in this world. There has to be a lot of beliefs because each individual creates a reality that prevents us from making the choice (to detach from physicality). People have to come to realize that a lot of what we believe to be true, is only true in *this* world. In the greater expanse of consciousness, in the greater expanse of reality, it's not true. It is only true for us because we make a choice for it to be true in order to participate physically.

S: It's all fascinating. What about all the information that came through about the electricity? Wasn't that fascinating?

GR: Yes. That floored me. I kept seeing the experiment where they have the bowl and the rocks and the centerpiece, and when they hooked up the wires to the motor, the motor runs. I could not for the life of me, figure out what kind of physical principle could explain that. And we can come up with whatever physical principle we want because that is not what is actually happening. Our universe expands outward with consciousness, and consciousness expands outward until it reaches the Source, the light source, and the Living Light. Both things are happening at the same time. In that case, 20 years ago, maybe, or not even that long ago, the "free energy" experiment could not have worked. It's happening now because consciousness has influenced physical properties.

It's like when magic was in existence. It continued for one moment in time in our history and became part of our consciousness. But because of the First Principle, physical reality was changing and the laws of physics changed too. The physical law of magic, the energy of mana, changed, too. It's no longer accessible to us, but it's still there. It's not destroyed.

S: We closed the door on it?

GR: Well, it got closed on us. We had no choice. Now we think of magic as a bunch of hand and mind tricks. That is the same thing that is going to happen in the future, even in this world, because you cannot stop that expansion no matter how many millions of us put on the brakes. We can make it come a little slower, but the new principles of consciousness are moving. Rather, the ever-expanding consciousness is now changing the principles of physics that we live in. So, the future world may laugh at us about "free energy" because for them, it will be right there instantly, already, as a "given". For us, we are just now finding it. We are still exploring it. And there are so many people that do not even believe in it because it's not part of their consciousness, not yet.

While we were talking this through, I was thinking, that other people experience the celestial side. I do not know how much of that Dolores Cannon deals with, I mean Ashtar, or celestial beings, or angelic beings.

S: They call them Ascended masters.

GR: They are all part of the drama. They are a little bit more liberated than we are.

S: Still part of the game that is going on here?

GR: And that stream of expanding consciousness and expanding physical world involves them, too. They do not escape it. We do not escape it.

S: Yes, yes. This was great. Thank you.

I called Grapo a few days after the second session and asked him to give his description of the First Principle. Here is what he said.

GR: The First Principle is absolute existence. In the beginning, there was light, and there was physical creation and simultaneously an expansion of consciousness. As we evolve, we are not evolving on our own through physical expansion. The consciousness expansion is driving us. It's the motivating force. The motivator is the Living Light, from the Source. We are striving to reach Source. It's an unstoppable flow; nothing stops it.

That is why you can apply brakes, slow down and experience this world and all of creation but you are still always moving in that direction, constantly.

The First Principle is the absolute reality of that stream of movement from the beginning of creation to the Source. That whole process of going from the Big Bang to light, to consciousness and to the Source. That is the First Principle. That is the most important thing. That is the absolute. That is the thing without questions.

What do we mean by "slowing down the stream?" We do not and can not slow the stream of light. Slowing down the stream is a metaphor for changing focus, it is a change of perspective. Coalescing out of the stream does not mean you leave the stream, it means your perspective changes from one of wholeness to a pinpoint focus.

A canon of the First Principle would be that mankind focus on achieving the return to that Source by whatever means we can.

CHAPTER 3
OUR JOURNEY NEEDS A GUIDE

Session 3: Travel on the Path

*W*e've asked the Guides to tell us about traveling though the Creation by using the power of consciousness. Grapo comes off the cloud and finds himself in a cellar.

GR: It's like a wine cellar, there are tables and chairs. Candles light the room. I feel this is a place I'm visiting as a traveler stopping by. I do not see anyone else. I am alone.

I took him fast forward to the next place.

GR: It's late at night. I am outside but not going anywhere. It seems to be a way station. I am waiting there. I get the impression of a vast wilderness all around. It's not easy to get from one place to another. Infinite space.

GHS: It's not easy for you to get from one place to another. Death in this world makes it difficult to contact the Source. You cannot cross the final line or border into Source.

The journey takes a long time. If we walk the path one step at a time, it takes forever. That is why we have those who come to help you and facilitate your journey. The progression is not spontaneous. It would be easy to get lost if we did not give assistance. Grapo is calling for assistance. We are demonstrating the difficulty of the task, considering the distance. This is why souls have contact with us. We can facilitate travel, but without us it would be too difficult.

S: Who are you?

G: The Guides. Sometimes it's necessary for people to struggle, so they understand that it cannot be done without us. A surrendering takes place during an intense struggle. It's easier to welcome the Guides than try to do it all by yourselves. It is a relationship. The distance is complex. Considering the depth of the travel that is required, traveling from place to place is too difficult without help.

It's not a veil of some other reality. We have to travel through reality. This is way more complex than you can appreciate when operating from the physical perspective. Pin-point focus lacks depth by definition. Things are done in a certain way because of the complexity and the depth of the journey.

GR: Is this life a lesson that has to be learned?

G: No. To wish upon a star is not the way to get there. Permission is not necessary. We see that he wishes to understand the process. It is infinitely more complex.

He asked for this understanding. The Guides create the path. He wishes to experience the complexity, but he cannot move forward. This is what he wants to know.

Grapo pops back into present time reality.

GR: I think this is all we are going to get. I think we asked the wrong question. We were asking about the process to learn how to get from one point to another. It's not singularly driven by us. No processes will work. That is why we have an assistant or Guides to help us through the process. Still having the five senses, we cannot get out easily because we see or experience or fathom the vastness of creation we are trying to get through.

I could see that it was nighttime, and it was like a way station. I was waiting to go, and they were saying, "Well, you chose to go by free will, and this is what you have to go through. It was really dense. It was like taking a journey through a thousand worlds by taking one step at a time. They said: "This is part of the creation process. This is part of where you exist, and you have to travel through it to get to the Source. That is why there are Guides and teachers, because they open up a path for you to travel."

I was learning what I needed to learn, basically, that you do not do it by yourself. You do not do it by willing it. There has to be an open cooperation between the two. I cannot just say, "Okay, I am willing to cooperate." They have to be saying it at the same time. That is the lesson. We asked for the process of travel, and they gave me an experience of the process without assistance. They wanted to make it clear that it's not done solely by you. This was not a case of being denied. It was a case of experiencing what it's like without a Guide, without their assistance.

In turn, that answers a lot of questions. Using a travel technique does not mean you are actually traveling through a great distance. The technique is actually communicating with the Guides to help you connect with them, so they can help you to contact Source.

It's not like we have been bad, and therefore cannot go. It's just that we do not understand the great depth and complexity. They left me at this way station, like a stagecoach way station. It's two or three in the morning, and there was a huge dark forest. They said: "Okay, travel the infinite distance, let's see what you can do." I looked at them, kind of dumbstruck and I said, "That is why I am asking."

They said, "You can ask all you like, but that is not what you asked originally. You asked to know and have the experience of going from point A to point B. We are teaching you that going from point A to point B is not by sheer will. It requires assistance. You cannot do it alone from a conscious level."

I guess you do it on a heart level, too. That answers some questions I had in the back of my mind about why is it not spontaneous continuously. It's because that path is not open, and we cannot force it open. We cannot design an instant formula for figuring out how to go from here to there. It's too complex.

This is not a punishment in any sense. They are not denying our travel. We can go, if we ask, but their assistance here is showing me why the process exists, why we cannot do it by sheer will, all by ourselves, without intermediaries or without Guides.

If we travel by forcing it through sheer will, we have to go through each world, each dimension, and each level of reality. Because of our five senses, it becomes more concrete as we travel. Our senses try to grab that fascinating reality, and it bogs us down. It does not get us very far.

S: Well, I would say that was a huge piece to experience.

GR: I guess, in a way, you are right because when we do our techniques, whether it's meditation or hypnosis or Reiki. Whichever technique we use, we get this impression that it's supposed to be easy and spontaneous because we have that technique. But it's not as easy and spontaneous as we think it is. We get the experience, and we say, "Ah ha! It was easy, but it was not. What we do not see are all the processes behind getting us there. That is why they said, "If you want an easy technique, its not going to happen because of the vastness of Creation."

From their perspective to our perspective is an infinite journey because there are worlds after worlds after worlds, and because we do not know those worlds. We do not even know those dimensions. We get lost. It's really easy to get bogged down. I have never really thought of it that way before.

S: So, we got something new today.

GR: Yeah, interesting. I now think Dolores Cannon's students get all those experiences, but they have a great deal of help.

S: Oh, absolutely. We've all witnessed that. I am not doing anything more than providing a space for something to happen. I depend on the Guidance for leading me to ask questions that will help, even if it's not what we think we want.

GR: You know, I was silent for a long time because part of me was waiting for that process to happen, and the process was never going to happen. It's kind of a dirty trick, but that's how I learned the lesson. So, part of my question was answered. There is no easy technique; there is no shortcut or forcing things through sheer will. It's like wanting to swim through the valley when you have to swim the entire distance through mud. I was not expecting that. It seems that the techniques we use are meant to help us get out of the mind and be able to connect with the Guides. We have to get out of the way and listen.

I wish I could relate what it was like being at the way station at "o-dark-thirty" in the morning, that sense of frustration, because of the depth of the wilderness before me. I was a total stranger in the middle of nowhere, and they were saying: "Well, this is what happens if you think you are so evolved that you can travel through the cosmos all by yourself. Go ahead and enjoy yourself." The funny thing was that I kept thinking, "When is the stage coach going to get here?" [Laughter.]

G: Oh, well, you did not ask for a stagecoach, you asked to do it all by yourself. You wanted to understand why you could not go from A to B. This is your lesson.

CHAPTER 4

DISEASE IS NOT A
PUNISHMENT

*B*efore *our session started, Grapo talked about needing his subconscious to reassure him and give him more confidence in preparation for his upcoming surgery.*

GR: So, what did you have in mind for this session?

S: You said on the phone you were scared about the surgery?

GR: Well, yes, I am apprehensive and scared. The last surgery I had was some 15 -20 years ago on my gallbladder. Basically, I went to the hospital alone. I didn't have any family support at the time, so I didn't really take the drugs the way I should have. When I was younger, you toughed through the pain. It was a guy thing. And it was so unbelievably painful. Part of the issue was that by the time I had gone in for surgery, I could no longer lay down flat because my spine is a little bit curved. I do not know what the surgery tables here on Kauai look like, but in those days as table was a flat piece of steel with a couple of steel wings that open up where you can put your arms out, for all the drug stuff.

S: Sounds a little like an angel wing spread.

GR: Or crucifixion. There were no pillows or anything like that. I was half drugged by the time I got to the operating room, and I could not tell them how uncomfortable I felt. So, I spent the whole 2 hour surgery on that flat metal table. I felt crucified on that table. When I came out of surgery and regained consciousness, all I could feel was searing pain in my shoulders and arms — from the table. It had nothing to do with the surgery. I remember one nurse in the post-operative ward. She brought in cinnamon graham crackers as a treat. She took good care of me. The staff kept trying to set me up with her for a date the whole time. It was funny. A sense of humor is the only thing that got me through that whole process.

S: Okay. So, now we want to get something from your higher self that will help you be more relaxed about the upcoming surgery, so you feel more confident about it.

GR: Yes. I remember that when I was a kid on Kauai, before they put in the first paved road to the airport, I knew Dr. Wilcox because he was the head doctor here. I do not think he made enough money though, because I was under the strange impression that when we little kids had our hair cuts on weekends —you know, bowl-shaped haircuts — he was the barber. I look back on that memory now and see it was ridiculous. Why would a surgeon do barber's work on the weekends? I do not know if there is any truth to it. I am saying this because when I was in a hallway at Wilcox Hospital recently, looking at the pictures of all the doctors, I realized my memory couldn't be true. It must be something I made up.

S: Well, who knows? People do very interesting things.

GR: Maybe they were not all that organized in those days. I do not know.

S: Well, the point is that you want to get some support for the surgery now. Have you talked with your doctor about this?

GR: No. I had an appointment with her nurse, a young man. I cannot remember his name, but I got sick, starting the day before, and I ended up in the emergency room. That screwed everything up. The nurses at the infusion center sent messages. I have only seen the doctor once before. She's the only oncologist on the island. The other doctor decided to work only on Oahu, not fly back and forth any more. It was getting on his nerves.

S: Are you going to talk with her and tell her about your past experience with surgery, tell her what you are concerned about, and let her tell you more what is the new scene for surgeries?

GR: Well, you know, she's the one who originally did my endoscope, when she told me I had cancer after the procedure. She's a really nice lady. She said to try to get the surgery on Oahu because they do colon surgery often. Here they do not do it very often, maybe once or twice a year. So I was apprehensive about getting a doctor here, but it turns out she is the doctor for me now, and I am comfortable with going to see her again.

S: Well, it's important to feel comfortable with your surgeon.

G: She's mainly a radiation oncologist. I have seen her every week, not like the other doctors, and she recommended a surgeon, a woman surgeon on Oahu, but apparently she doesn't take my insurance. It's not going to happen with her on Oahu. Well, that is the way it goes. I am resigned to working with the doctor here. I like her. She's funny.

S: That's good.

GR: She's funny, and she has a kind of strength about her. Really good common sense, too. I am not uncomfortable with having her do the surgery. It's just that every time I go in for some procedure where they put you to sleep, I get nervous. I didn't realize there are two different types of putting you to sleep. In one type, they give you a drug to put you to sleep. In the other type, mostly when they do major surgery, they put a tube down your throat into your lungs, in case you stop breathing, and they can force you to breath. I do not like the thought of that. Anything that goes into my throat scares me. Other than the table, the one thing I remember about the last surgery was that my throat was on fire because I was so scared, and they do not want to give you any water. They did not want my body to start functioning too fast. They want me to revive slowly, so it takes time. I was begging for ice, but when I get the ice, it was too hard to swallow any kind of water. Catch 22.

S: Hopefully it's better now than it used to be.

GR: I hope so too. I am hoping their techniques have gotten a lot better.

S: I have had several surgeries myself, and it's an opportunity, really. You can have entertainment the whole time if you relax enough. No resistance. They give you the drugs, and you are out. You can go play. If you are ready, you can remember what happened while you were under the anesthetic. Most people do not relax and ask for an adventure. They do not remember what happened when they come back into their everyday life again.

GR: I remember when they took out my tonsils as a kid. In those days, they used ether. I woke up in the middle of the surgery, consciously woke up, and I remember the anesthesiologist trying to put me back to sleep.

S: It's quite different now than when we were kids.

GR: So, what else did you want to delve into?

S: Your surgery is the main thing, but is there something else that you have been thinking about or wanting?

GR: I was thinking about what I should ask. My general focus is bringing out the knowledge the Guides want us to bring out. Maybe it's a new translation or a new view they want. I do not want to be consciously looking only for the answers that I want. I would rather be the in-between person.

S: Sometimes the Guides are silent, waiting until they get the right question.

GR: They are always there, whether I know it or not. So, I am hoping this time we leave it up to them to decide.

S: Okay. That is probably the best thing at this point. I listened again yesterday to most of the second session. It helped me to integrate a bit more. The Guides said that when we step into the whole earth creation, it's stepping out of the flow of the evolution. We get slowed down while we explore life on this earth. This is a very interesting exploration. I can see why we want to step off the train and find out what is going on here. But once we step off the train, we say, "Oh, my God! I didn't realize it was this painful."

GR: Surprise.

S: Then we got caught up in it. We are curious to see whatever else is going on.

GR: Yeah.

S: So, when I think about what you've presented, there are two parts to it. There is the part of how we got here in the first place, and then there is the part about how much more is out there that we have no clue about, and *that* is where we are *really* going.

GR: Uh-huh. One of the things I found interesting about that session was not so much how difficult life can be, but that you do not and can not do it alone. A lot of New Age people, when all this light transmission first came in, were all talking about "ascension," elevating their consciousness or going to some city in the sky, or whatever it was. That is their desire, but maybe that is not the process. The Guides were saying to them, "Wait a minute. Just because you are having all these different experiences does not necessarily mean that is what you are going to get. We are behind all of your experiences. We are guiding you. And you are not going to get what you think you are going to get." Basically, every time there is a new wave of energy coming in, people get all disappointed because they do not get what they are looking for. They get what they need.

S: Right.

GR: I remember I used to listen to a group that channeled the Ashtar Command. It was a really nice group, and they had really nice things to say, but what they said never really came out like they were thinking it was going to come out. Finally, I read this thing on the Internet from the Ashtar saying, "Why are you thinking we are going to come down and save you? We do not interfere in your planet. We do not interfere in anything. The only thing we do, every 50 years, is align ourselves with the energy that helps to support you. That is all we do." I bet that disappointed a lot of people. To me, why would you be an enlightened being and want to come down and mess things up more, you know?

S: Yeah.

GR: There must be varying degrees of enlightenment up there, as well, if you really think about it. I am sure they have good intentions, but.... Daren was telling me about a guy who channels the Akashic records. He had something like 20 episodes up on YouTube. He talked about the history of the universe as far as earth is concerned, why certain things happen, why certain Beings do certain things. It all sounded a little too contorted. "Get to the point," I said to Daren, "because I do not have to believe everything he says." Basically, he was saying that although Beings of higher intelligence come to support us, they are not really supporting us. They are supporting themselves because they do not have the means of experiencing the physical experiences we do. They come down and say they are here to help us, but really they just farm us for experiences they can integrate into their own DNA, so they can have our experience, our knowledge of what is going on. Isn't that against the "prime directive" or something?

Okay, so there are different levels of intelligent Beings. I am interested only because I want to know the structure of that space society. I am curious, but that is not where I want to end up. My focus is on consciousness development and spiritual development.

S: Because we've been doing this communication with the Guides, and it's opening new doorways, has it given you any feeling that, well, you really want to see how this life is going to turn out, so you better stay a while?

GR: Here?

S: Yeah.

GR: No, no.

S: You are ready go?

G: I cannot say I am ready, but I cannot say I am not ready. I am kind of ambivalent. I know that I am going. That is not a question anymore. I know that I am going sometime. How soon is hard to tell.

S: That would be true for all of us.

GR: It is. Maybe when we transition into another body, into another world, we cannot get the same concept of time. I mean, a Martian concept of time would be totally different from a Venusian concept, or something like that. If beings exist on those planets and if they are conscious, since spiritual evolution is different, it's not that they do not understand us, they may be just looking at us and saying how primitive we are.

S: Got that.

GR: However, Daren seems to think it's really the opposite, that this is the jewel world. We can get experiences here that no other planet can. Well, I understand that philosophy, but there is a part of me that asks, why only here? Why is it a hundred percent here and only 99 percent somewhere else? Why not a hundred percent everywhere?

S: In your second session, you said that we chose to forget. It wasn't that we had to forget, but it was going to give us a more unique experience if we did forget. So, we said yeah, let's forget so we can really get what this is about on the earth.

GR: I once had a session about me experiencing who I am. In a larger sense. I am a traveler from a world that is totally energetic. I was sent out from my light world to travel to different worlds in this physical reality. I was supposed to be observing only. I was never to interfere with anything. So, I think we overshot that belief when we came into this world, because this world is all about interfering. You can choose to interfere with what is going on here. You know, the Heisenberg principle [the Observer Effect]. If you look at what is going on, you change what is going on because you are part of the process now.

Basically, I was sent here to observe and experience. All that knowledge is being transmitted continuously back to my home world, so the greater body of our civilization would understand what is going on. They sent us all over the universe. There was no concept of age. I got the impression that I was already hundreds of thousands of years old.

The best part of that session was that I made a connection with the Guide, the teacher, who took me from my home world. They assign an elder to each individual, and there was this woman who took me throughout the universe and then left me alone for many hundreds of years. She had tutored me on how to have experiences, but I got to the point that I graduated. She was no longer necessary, so she left. When I had that session, I re-established contact with her. It was like pure joy, pure bliss, because she was appreciating my existence, and I could appreciate my home world. That was a mind-blowing experience.

S: It appears the Guides are showing you that your "home world," that energetic world, is still a part of you and Creation.

GR: Yeah, it is.

S: This time you are going further than that. You are going outside the whole thing to go all the way back to source or origin.

GR: Yeah. We are already celestial beings, in this world, trying to escape back beyond the celestial world.

S: Okay, well, I want to make sure that you are getting adequate support for the surgery, so you'll be able to let go of any attachment to what is going to happen in the surgery or anything else.

GR: I keep reading up on Hashimoto's disease, which is a thyroid immune system disorder.

S: My mother had that.

GR: Eighty percent of thyroid disease is Hashimoto's. It's a thyroid dysfunction connected to immune sensitivity. That is why I have digestion issues. The intestines are all about immunity. The other thing I kept bumping into is that the dysfunction has to do with the communication processes inside the body. This is really odd, when you think about it. I am from a world where the whole process is communications.

S: But you spent so much time being an observer, so obviously because of what we are doing together, this is the time to let it out. This is something for me to share with you. I also was born with low thyroid. For me it was like I had an unseen snake around my neck that was blocking out information from the outside and protecting me, like a buffer between me and the world. I was pretty dumbed down when I was growing up. I didn't get the low thyroid identified until I was 37 years old. When I finally got some thyroid support it changed my life. I woke up to a lot of what was going on around here.

GR: That's interesting because I see the process I went through as the reverse. When I was a young kid, I already consciously knew about creation and about God. There wasn't any need to tell me about God because it was like preaching to the choir. Then I got shut down because my father was alcoholic. My whole family was dysfunctional. I came in a little more enlightened, but I got dumbed down. My consciousness was squashed. All my intuition was squashed. By the time I was in high school, I was thinking of myself as a scientist. That was when I met Daren, I think I was a senior, and she got me started in learning meditation.

She was a teacher at the time with her first husband. I bless that day because meditation, the TM technique, took me away from all those things I believed about myself, threw it away, and let me be quiet and peaceful for the first time in my life since I was a kid, back when I felt connected to God. I realized there was another aspect of me in a state of peace, not in a state of confusion. It was not a state of feeling socially awkward because my father was an alcoholic or because my mother and father divorced when I was really young.

I final got to the point where I said, "There is another me here, and it's not the old me." That was my liberation in this world. I final got in contact with myself. All of a sudden, I turned around and looked around, and I said, "My life is not that miserable." Life can be fun. I can enjoy doing things because I was taken out of that place where I could not focus, where I did not understand what was going on or why this was happening to me. So, learning mediation was one of my biggest blessings in this world.

S: What about the Hashimoto's disease. Did you have surgery for that?

GR: No.

S: But you take supplements?

GR: I take Synthroid, which mimics some of the lost hormones, but there is no cure for Hashimoto's disease. In order to resolve the Hashimoto's disease issues, the immunity issues, I saw a Vietnamese doctor who told me that my thyroid issues, my stomach distress, my kidney problems, is all part of the cancer and related to Hashimoto's. It's hard to deal with the Hashimoto's disease because all these added immune diseases started developing. The doctor said I have to support my thyroid, and I have to redevelop my immune system, but until that is done, the Hashimoto's won't heal itself.

In trying to find out how to do all that, one of the things I found out is that wheat gluten mimics thyroid tissue. Many people are allergic to gluten. When I eat gluten, my body's immune system goes into attack mode, and attacks the thyroid because my body thinks I've increased the amount of thyroid tissue. My body automatically starts doing what it's supposed to be doing. But the result is that my body self-destructs.

S: My mother said, " I am allergic to my own thyroid." She took Synthroid. She also had a surgery to deal with thyroid tissue that was strangling her.

GR: It's almost like a cancer, but it's not cancer. Some people have to have the thyroid gland completely removed. I am not at that point, mainly because I got thyroid support early on. But I must have been low thyroid for years before they figured it out. Now my real issue is how to deal with the worsening of the Hashimoto's disease, the loss of immunity, which is a catch 22 because radiation knocks out the immunity. So, I am sticking to a very restricted diet, no gluten of any kind, such as no egg protein because egg whites have gluten, too. I can eat rice, and vegetables. A lot of vegetables have to be cooked, like broccoli and cabbage, because those vegetables have an enzyme that slows down the functioning of the thyroid, so it does not help to eat it raw.

I cannot eat any soy-based products, either. Soy interferes with the thyroid gland. I was a vegetarian for a while, and my main focus was on soy products. I love Japanese foods, which is chocked full of soy, whether soy sauce or whatever. I was doing all these things to help myself, but I was doing it all backwards.

S: One of the things that make me angry is that we get this food information, and we think we are doing the best thing, but it turns out that it's not correct.

GR: That's part of the confusion. From all my bloating and gas and pain, they found the colon cancer. And I said, "Oh, I am getting it from three different directions."

S: Right.

GR: I am basically saying, let's deal with the most important one right now, then we'll deal with the second most important one, and slowly try to cure the Hashimoto's disease by getting the body's health back. By the same token, I'm getting the message that it's not Hashimoto's either, because the doctors are working on me, and that's causing side effects.

S: Yeah, yeah,

GR: So, like I said, it's all a catch 22. I am getting hit no matter which direction I turn, and that's frustrating. As bad as things are, what do I do? I got infected with stomach bacteria, and that was horrific. That was why I ended up in the hospital. My intestinal flora was totally out of whack. You can you pick up these bugs in doctors offices and hospitals, so I went to see my general practitioner, and I picked up the disease. I was on antibiotics of one type or another for three days.

S: I asked the question when I was a little kid, why don't doctors get sick. I think there is something in our soul plan that puts us in those places, and we allow it in.

GR: Who knows what that is all about, but it's serving us in some way. My Guidance said to go ahead and go to the hospital, do the chemo and everything else, because it's part of my process, and it's okay. The Guides said to relax and enjoy the process. My immune system is already compromised, so whatever bug looks at me is going to get me.

S: I guess we put out a welcome flag. We say, I am going into this place because if I allow a bug into my body, it's going to do something that ultimately is going to be for my well being for that bug to exist in this body.

GR: I agree with that in one sense, but in another sense, part of that philosophy kind of saved me. I see things from a larger perspective, looking down. Higher consciousness already knows what is good, what is perfect. Part of me is saying, "No, we are not going to do this as a game plan because we know better." But being stuck in this environment, so to speak, whether you are stuck or not, you are going to have to play the game that is here.

Part of me is saying, "No, this is not your lesson plan. It does not matter if you get cancer and another person loses an arm or a leg in a war. That is just part of the process in this world." But when I look at this and say it's my lesson plan, it's accepting that reality. And part of me says I cannot accept that reality, that it's not my reality. It's the reality of this world. I cannot identify with it. That is why I chafe at people saying, "You are a co-creator." That annoys me.

S: I thought that is what I said. I am not sure where the miscommunication is.

GR: It's not miscommunication. It's the way it's phrased. In one sense, when you say you are a co-creator, or it's your lesson plan, there is almost an inherent idea that this is what you have to go through. But that is not the truth. You do not have to get through it or go through it if — and this is the big rub — if you are enlightened enough and aware enough of what reality is all about. You get to go through it and accept it as your lesson plan, if you choose, but only if I do not see it from the other side.

S: That's what the Guidance was telling you, that this is not the lesson?

GR: Right.

S: And this disease process is not a punishment?

GR: No, it is not.

S: Is that a skewed perspective - the idea that we have to learn a lesson?

GR: It's skewed because of the perspective we are seeing from. From a higher perspective, Source consciousness, unity insures your consciousness of greater wholeness. I do not see it the same way. I do not see from this world out. I see from the higher world into this world. That's why they said the First Principle is the most important of all because it tries to get the individual back on that path of loving light. Doing that raises your consciousness, so you can see from that perspective. Without seeing from that perspective, you can get caught in this reality very easily. That is why they said choices are not a gift. Choices gave you a break, a physical break, to stop and slow you down. These lead you into all kinds of other choices; all kinds of brakes to slow you down and change your perspective.

They said mankind really didn't fall with the angels. What happened is that mankind turned away from the light. They didn't fall from grace. They were always in grace, but they do not perceive it because they looked away from the Living Light. That is a different perspective.

When people say, it's your lesson plan, or you are a co-creator, that indicates you have no connection in some sense with higher consciousness. In some philosophical sense, maybe you do not. But in absolute reality, that is who you are. You have to look at it from that perspective, or you will see these people going around saying, "Oh, my God. I am suffering. God, why did you do it to me? God, why do you not help me?" First, God didn't do it to you. God gave you the gift to let you help yourself. If you want to return to the presence of being with God, then you have to go back to your Source. You have to raise your consciousness. Then you can understand that God didn't do anything to you, you did it to yourself. All these choices put on the brakes and stop you from doing so. So, perspective is very important. I think that part of the First Principle is perspective. They want you to go back to the original perspective — wholeness, the experience of living love.

S: Everybody is headed in that direction, but to finally get there, you have to get out of this bubble of creation that includes all these universes and realities and levels.

GR: You have to stop making choices in this world.

S: And really get back into the flow of going Home?

GR: Right. Because the process of being in the Living Light and progressing to the Source never stops. It's our perception.

S: But we put on the brakes. We said we are going to go into this creation and see what this life is all about?

GR: Exactly. But if mankind can get the concept of the First Principle, it won't be trying so hard. For instance, they won't develop the slowing down process of religion, which does not help. Religion codifies what does not need to be codified. It makes concrete now of energies that might not have to be concrete five or ten years from now.

You must come to a universal understanding of what is going on, and go forward from there even though you are still in this world. You are going to make different choices if you see life from that perspective. If you say, "This is my lesson plan, and that is my fate," that's just another form of putting on the brakes. If you say, "Oh, I don't have to go through this," then you really do not have to go through it.

What I love the best about the Tantra tradition and the Bhagavad Gita is that they say getting to higher consciousness is not a question of meditating every day, every day, every day. It's a question of meditating and in one of those experiences, you turn around and see from the other perspective, and the "Ah ha!" awakens your consciousness. That is all you really need.

Meditation is a tool, like a ladder to get to the top. It's not the beginning or the end of the process. You use it until you are done with it. Then you enter different levels of consciousness, and your tool changes. You cannot say, "I have reached a certain state of consciousness, so I am going to keep using this tool because that is where I want to be." You have to let that tool go and expand into the next level of consciousness. Consciousness changes.

So whenever people say, "in the lesson plan you are co-creating..." to me, that is like somebody slapping on the biggest hand brake you can find. If anything, we need to get away from that. Liberation, that is the thing I like about Buddhism. I am sure I have been a Buddhist many times over. Buddha took away the religious aspect. It became a science of the mind. People still think it's a physical process, like in the Tantric tradition, due to the sutras, so they see Buddhism as religion, where it's not only a religion. It's unified mind consciousness — the mind/body relationship. This is why there is a difference between a Tantric understanding and the Hindu understanding, with Vedanta practices, the Bhagavad-Gita and everything else. Hinduism was developed from the priestly Brahmin rituals. The absolute reality is that you do not need a priest. You do not need anybody else. You might find people who help you get to where you are going, but once you see that you are your own teacher, your own inner guidance is there to help you with higher consciousness.

In my own mind I am trying to get people to say stop looking for the brakes. Let all that stuff go. What you are trying to achieve is way beyond all those physical and conscious realities. Who knows what consciousness is like when you are in the extreme of the body. In the presence of the Source, everybody can explain its worth. Source energy is full of love, and the energy is so intense.

Sometimes when we are doing these sessions, if I stop and my body shakes, it's because I am really close to that spiritual energy, and it's affecting my physical body. So, what I want from higher consciousness, or the Source, is for the Guides to bring into our world that which would bring clarity, so we can stop shooting ourselves in our collective foot. Yes, you can do it by going from this experience to that experience, from this religion to that philosophy, but I think there is a clearer way that the Guides can offer us. That is what I am hoping. Maybe there does not have to be 5,000 steps to enlightenment, you know?

S: Yeah.

GR: Maybe there is only a hundred or twenty.

S: Okay.

GR: In these sessions, Guidance said, they are in control. They are the ones who are going to show us the experiences we need to know. Well, I think they cannot come to us and tell us what to do, like Moses and the burning bush. They cannot just give us the command because that isn't going to happen, partly because of the way reality and consciousness is set up. It's too difficult for us on this level to go to where we really want to go, back to the Source. There are other places, other worlds, that are incredibly more enlightened than we are, and people are more in their spiritual bodies than they are in a physical body; but even they have to go through a process.

S: They are still in that big bubble called Creation.

GR: Right.

S: So, popping out of the big bubble, that is what you are engaged in. And when we talk from this side about what is called death, it means death within this creation?

GR: Right.

S: So, all the karma, the religious ideas, the different gods, the rebirth, and all of that is still in this creation. But the First Principle is where consciousness and the whole flow of expansion is going, is this a bursting out of that creation bubble?

GR: Right.

S: To go all the way. So, that is what ascension is.

GR: Yeah. That is the ascension.

S: Instead of transitions?

G: Yes. Ascension is not about being with the ascended masters, it means transcending everything, going back to the Source.

S: Yeah.

GR: It's hard for me to listen now to the News Agers. They have great intentions. They have such great desires to return to Source, but they do not know what Source is. They say the Source of it is love. Well, it's a great deal more. We cannot express that here because we do not have that consciousness yet. So, we grab on to the nearest thing we can to it. This is our liberation. We are going to this place that is freer than our current place, but then we have to go to another place. Each step makes it a little bit easier, but it's still difficult because you are seeing so many pictures, so many different perspectives. I think the First Principle is telling us that there is only one perspective.

One of the things the Hashimoto's disease does, it raises your body temperature. That is why I like cold places. That is why I dream about cold places. I do not dream about desserts or the Midwest. I dream that I am in a cold place. I cannot be there in a physical body that is always heating up, always burning itself up. I am hoping the Guides can come through and give us some clarity on this, to get to a certain level of consciousness that can contact higher consciousness.

If there are 20 people in an audience, and I say to go to XYZ, they go to one place, which is fine, but there are still problems. If I say, go to #5, and you'll cut through XYZ, you'll cut through all the rigmarole you think you have to learn. You cut through your lesson plan because you are returning directly to the Source. That is what I am hoping to do for us through recording and publishing these sessions.

S: So, the Guides are showing you pictures or taking you through experiences, and then you are able to report it. It's almost as though so much happens that what you report afterwards in our debrief is even more fulfilling, from my perspective.

GR: When I go to that level of consciousness, and higher consciousness starts speaking, I notice there is a part of me that has always desired to contact the Source.

S: Is that part of your attachment, the part that you need to relax out of it?

GR: Right. But my experiences with this have been so profound so far, and even this much is overwhelming, because consciousness takes on a different perspective for me. When I contact Source, or the Living Light, the extreme of it is another level of refined consciousness. I can speak from that other level of refined consciousness, or rather, higher self speaks from that level. What happens is that you ask a question, and I can feel a smile coming to my lips because I not only understand what you are asking but I understand the depth of where your question comes from, where I am, and I can see how you would ask that question, but if you were in my place, the question would be totally irrelevant.

S: Yeah?

GR: The Living Light has a sense of humor that can look back at this world and smile.

S: Uh huh.

GR: It's the desire we have to help others that is helping us to stop, that is putting on the brakes, such as helping you in this project. I am willing to do this for that reason and that reason alone. I am not looking for my name on any book, and I do not want to be identified by the public as this guy who did these sessions.

S: Yeah. I understand that.

GR: Public recognition is totally irrelevant. It's the clarity of these sessions that is important.

S: Yes, I agree.

GR: Before we get started. Did you visit that website site I sent to you about the guy who had the near death experience [mellen-thomas.com].

S: Yes.

GR: Didn't you find his stuff fascinating? It's a different perspective. Mellen didn't want to die, so he came back with a different attitude. He describes the stream of light strapped to the universe, the Source. His essential Guide was great.

I think Mellen was lucky in the sense that he knew, his Source knew, that he was going to die. At the last minute, he made the choice that he did not want to die. You always have that choice. So, Mellen was really happy when he came back because he didn't have to die. He told his story from that perspective, from not having to die. I thought that was really fascinating because we have the same story but from different perspectives.

S: Okay. Well, shall we get started?

GR: Yeah.

CHAPTER 5

THE POWER OF PERSPECTIVE

Session 4: The Train to Singularity

GHS: I see a small barn. I am feeling that animals were there, but now they are gone. It is kind of musty. There is a small fenced area out front, surrounded by trees. Feels like I am abandoned there. Now, there is someone standing by the fence. He looks kind of like a cowboy.

S: Do you recognize this person?

GHS: No. It's not the one I have met before.

S: I'd like you to look down at your own feet. See what kind of covering you have on your feet, or if you are barefooted.

GHS: I have boots on.

S: Are you dressed somewhat like that cowboy?

GHS: I do not really see myself dressed like the cowboy. He's wearing work clothes, cowboy boots. He's telling me, "We all *work the land.* We all *work the land* whether we are cowboys or farmers or towns people. We all *work the land.* "

S: Does that feel right to you, that you *work the land*?

GHS: I think he's using it as a metaphor.

S: Can you explain that metaphor for me?

GHS: He said we do all kinds of different jobs, but the job has the same focus. It does not matter whether you are an office worker or farmer or cowboy, because it's the same purpose. We all work for the same purpose.

S: Uh huh. And what do we do for the land with the work we do?

GHS: There is something connected between the earth and the Source. He seems to be saying there is a universal integration at peace with the earth, with the Source, all in the stream of life. People are attached to the land, attached to the earth. There is a degree of connectivity beyond our individual desires to stay in this world. It's something apart and beyond our own process.

S: Do we do this kind of a multitasking more often than we think?

GHS: It's another path, same perspective. We cannot see the whole yet. We get lost in the individuality of what we are doing. The concept of land here has a singularity about it. That is why people want to go to certain places away from their normal habitat, because they are tapping into that universal singularity.

S: As they travel, are they reinforcing that connection?

GHS: Yes. It allows them to disengage from daily activities. It allows them to walk away, so to speak, from their everyday activities, their small perspective, and to broaden their view.

As we move away from the stream of life, consciousness brings forth a different level of perspective. We begin to see individuals from the perspective of wholeness. Greater consciousness not only sees the whole, but also sees the individual aspects of consciousness expressing. We come to seek the perception of us being in the stream. It's like a great harmony for those of us who travel the stream. We reach out in singularity to see the individuals' small realities as a way for us to perceive other realities and other experiences without leaving the stream of life. It's not necessary to disengage from the stream of life, the flow of the universe.

We have choices and those choices change our perspective. We get caught up in the reality of other worlds. We lose our perspective of the whole, but we are not apart from that reality. It's perception, or continued singularity. We flow out of the stream of life with our senses, our awareness. With our other perceptions we reach out and touch outside of the singularity, outside of the stream of life. That which is outside the singularity of the stream of life is not unreal. It's not an illusion. It's part of our experience, but not as solid as we are soft. We are transparent. This is a different type of perception.

We are lost in a world of our own creating. We dream about worlds, and in each of these worlds, there is one singularity. We must travel away from one perspective to free ourselves from that vision, that reality, and we are more able to see our singularity in the stream of life. We never fall out of the stream of life. It's our perception, which flows out of the stream of life.

It's like riding a train. Your perception moves out of the train when you look out of the window and see the scenery, but you are still established in that singularity of riding in the train. You are using a different perspective to see out. Your perspective can become so focused that you make the vision you are seeing become as real as anything. This world has dominion, as the Source, as the stream, as in the singularity. For those who travel on land, when they move away from their individual soul perspective, they gain a continuance in that singularity. It becomes easier to see who they really are, what they really are.

S: That puts a whole new perspective on vacations and traveling.

GHS: A vacation of the mind is similar to a vacation of the soul. Traveling is looking away, looking away from the train we are in, looking away through the window and seeing scenery beyond. It's in this very process of looking away that you find yourself and lose yourself. They are one in the same process.

S: So is this one of the ways, then, that we let go of our attachments to our daily life?

GHS: Yes.

S: So, it's actually a spiritual thing we are doing when we take a vacation?

GHS: Yes. When you take a vacation, it's a vacation of the mind, away from the individuals' subtleties of life into another area of life. A vacation frees your perspective, if only temporarily. It's a soul journey, a turning away and looking back at the train that is the soul journey. Many people have the perspective that these worlds are illusions; but they are not illusions. They are all God's creation. Your perspective into Creation is what brings you experience. The creations are very powerful. They can lead you *away* from the singularity that we are. In the end you always become aware of our singularity, where we are. You stop looking out the window. You stop riding the train.

S: Is that when we get off the train and have a different experience?

GHS: No. The train is a perspective. The train is what is in our eyes as we look up from the stream of life. Mankind rides the small train of perspective in this reality. People need to ride the big train of perspective in this reality instead. That way when you look away, you see into the singularity. You see into the Source.

Creation was created to bring experience. It may bring us pain, but it does not bring us punishment. Each individual's reality, if that person has turned away from the light, is what brings punishment or suffering to that person. When we travel, we travel away from that perspective. We travel to the sea. We travel to the forest. This reminds us of looking out the window of that experience. It reminds us that we can look away, return to that singularity, to the Source. We can be one expression of the Source instead of many, many, expressions. This is the clarity we need you to have. It's the expression of the truth, the Oneness of the First Principle. It's how we journey. We are showing you this perspective to promote clarity and understanding.

S: This train analogy makes it possible for me to understand. I also feel in my body as though it's going to take some time for me to integrate this information. That is okay.

GHS: Yes. That is why I say we all *work the land,* or, *stand on the land.* We all stand on the train of perspective. We all stand in singularity. As we journey on the land, we journey in our perspective on that train, the stream of life that flows forth, our Source. We all stand in singularity. Nothing is unreal. Nothing is not real. A singularity stands outside of all creation. It's the expression beyond all creation. There is continuance in the movement forward and the movement towards the Source. There is continuance in moving from the city to the village, from the village to the mountains. Always remain clear that we are traveling on that train, moving us in the stream of life. That is our singularity. That is our contact with our singularity. That is our journey to the Source. All is movement forward. That is the First Principle.

S: What you are calling moving forward seems to me like it's an expansion in all directions. Is "forward" an idea in our linear reality, but the true expansion is in all directions?

GHS: The universe has movement. It has a beginning and end in the Source. We flow from one to the other. It's a perception of movement. It's the perception of being on a train and the choice to look out the window. It's the brakes we apply to see into smaller worlds. If we are also in singularity, where there is no movement, where all is one, we are all of the Creation at once, all possibilities, and all things. Only when we travel the stream of life outside the absolute reality of singularity do we become conscious of movement, become aware of direction.

S: Well, my mind is not able to quite get this. It seems you've been saying there really is no end. The universe is infinite and eternal yet it keeps moving and expanding?

GHS: The expression of a Source creation is in movement. It's only when you understand and experience the singularity that there is no movement.

S: So, for most humans on earth, this is the state they are in?

GHS: It's a state of all creation.

S: The big bubble of all creation?

GHS: Whether we are human, whether we are some other humanoid, whether we are celestial, all that exists is inside the expression of Source creation. But our true identity is outside in singularity, outside of the stream of life.

S: Well, it's very lovely to me that you, as Grapo's Guide, showed up today as a cowboy. Cowboys represent to us the frontier of the new, and it's very nice. Previously, Grapo was being shown that he needs his Guides to help him go through all the phases of the transition. Has he now kept that agreement, that connection with his Guides, with you, so that his transition is more in alignment?

GHS: The process is always in alignment. It's an individual perception that he is not capable of seeing that alignment which causes disruption.

S: So, have you been showing him that he is more compatible, guiding him on the way?

GHS: He has always been on the way. He has always been in Guidance. You are never outside of Guidance, even in the darkest times. Even in the process of death, you are always being guided. Even when you are lost, you are being guided.

S: That's reassuring.

GHS: You may not feel our hand holding yours, but we are always holding your hand. The sense of a child being lost is a loss of awareness. The child is not being lost as an individual. You are always whole. You are always part of the singularity.

S: So when you use the word *singularity*, is it the same meaning when I use the word *oneness*?

GHS: I use the word, but it's incomplete. I cannot describe the wholeness of the meaning down here, even from my perspective. It's a reality you cannot conceive.

S: As many times as I have been given the answer, "You wouldn't understand it from where you are," I still keep trying.

GHS: Yes.

S: And is it revealing more and more to us as we focus on this new way of perceiving things?

GHS: It's here to help you bring clarity.

S: I am very grateful for that, and I know Grapo is, too. One of the reasons we wanted to come together today was to support Grapo in his adventure into the world of surgery that will be coming up in the near future. He's had some residue fear from past surgeries of what it might be like. Can you give him some shift of his perspective on this process, so it will help him to ride through the surgery in greater comfort and ease, or whatever is needed for what we call a successful surgery?

GHS: He has chosen not to be aware of the details. He wants the process to be over.

S: Yes, he does.

GHS: He has associated the end process with pain, and there is a certain amount of pain that we will assist him with handling.

S: I am sure he's going to be very glad to hear that, to know that and feel it in his body, in his mind, that he has assistance from you to make it an easier journey. Is that process starting now, so that he can be more conscious of the assistance he is getting, so he can relax into it and be at peace with it?

GHS: Yes. That is why we bring clarity.

S: Okay. Good. Very good. Is there anything else you can communicate to him that will assist with the surgery?

GHS: Not at this time. Continue the process.

S: Very good. Thank you.

GHS: Be at peace.

CHAPTER 6
INDIVIDUAL CONSCIOUSNESS IN GROUPS

Discussion Before the Session

GR: I do not want myself to be the project. I want the stuff from higher consciousness to be the project.

S: You asked me if it was the higher self speaking about karma? Since my mother died, I have been able to talk with my mother through the computer. She comes in, and I type whatever comes up, so I am familiar with that way of doing it.

After hearing the information you are bringing in, given what I have already thought in the past and the things I am reading, I am thinking, "Wait a minute!" People are still stuck in this painful belief system that says they have to get payback for their mistakes. I must have done something really horrible, so I have to do this as karma thing. It does not make sense to me.

When I asked to communicate with my mother, it was so beautiful because when that shift in my awareness came, it was the same but not as deep. Even when I am typing, I can feel it, and I am not the one answering. My personality is not answering. There is something else feeding me this information. I always enjoy doing that a lot. I think that is probably going to increase now, with you. So, that is good.

GR: Yeah. On the way here, I was wondering why we need to turn something universal into a dogmatic form that is so concrete that it loses its truth after a while. In the time when Jesus was around, people had an opportunity to learn, but the Bible was not really written [or codified], they say, until after he'd been gone for about 200 years.

S: That would be accurate.

GR: What are they going to remember after 200 years?

S: The stories that were passed down.

GR: But I think it might be more than an issue of control and authority. I figure that on this level of consciousness, there seems to be a need to make information more meaningful, more real for the individual than it really is. There is a strong desire to do that.

If you look at what we have been hearing, if you look at a society that lives on that level, they are not running around practicing religion. So, religion, in a sense, is making concrete what is universal, but it loses its depth and its meaning when you do that. I wonder why humanity has a strong need to do that.

It's like in the Muslim community. They were not happy enough to be Muslim and live the teachings of Muhammad. They had to say, this is your Muhammad, and that is my Muhammad. They ended up with two different sects that are forever fighting one another. The same thing happened in Christianity between Catholics and Protestants. So, we have some need in humanity that has joined certainty to power and control and project it out as what is real or absolute. This is the way it *must* be.

S: You feel more secure to have religion when you are disconnected from source and yourself. You want something to rely on, so it's meeting the need, but I think everything is changing. People are becoming more connected, and as they feel more connected, they will not have the same needs. People are going to be able to allow other people to be different. I am so secure in myself that that I do not need you to believe what I believe. It's okay.

GR: So what do you have in mind that we do this time?

S: Well, I didn't have anything in mind. Last time we said we would leave it up to the higher self instead of trying to direct it, and it worked beautifully. And I know you love connecting with that place?

GR: Yes.

S: I did want to tell you how I go about contacting higher self and getting messages for myself. This is what is being opened up for everybody who is aware, and people can be doing it any time, on their own. But I love being together with you, so I want you to come and let me help. I want to be the facilitator who allows you to go to that deeper place, so you do not have to think about anything. You can just let it come through.

GR: I think I feel more of a sense of neutrality when we do it this way.

S: Yeah?

GR: Maybe I should learn to self hypnotize myself. I have always been interested in hypnosis, believe it or not, but I had never acted on it until about three years ago when I first did a Dolores Cannon session.

The odd thing was that I was the one who promoted it to Daren as a means of understanding higher consciousness. She was willing to go along with it because she has a lot of Guides, a lot of resources that come from somewhere else. They appear out of the blue for her. After the first session, she was the one that ended up going to Dolores Cannon to learn the technique, not me. She could not afford it, but her friends thought it was such a great idea, so they sent her. Daren has friends who think she is their emissary, so they send her all over the place, which is fine because she loves doing stuff like that.

I have not personally gotten involved with any community in the last 20 years. When I first learned to meditate in 1972, I was graduating from high school. My hopes and dreams were to get into a daily routine, the working world economy, although I had a lot of monk-like tendencies. I gained great understanding when I went to do the meditations, but there has always been a conflict in me whether to do the meditations and related techniques, or to go on with life, to be in the outside reality. I kept getting all these conflicting signals.

Friends kept telling me, "You are not really doing what you need to do, and there is a part of you trying to do something else. There is a part of you trying to express higher consciousness, and you are not listening." My desire was always to do both the outward stroke and the inward stroke, so there was kind of a conflict for a long time. Why am I not doing what I need to do to be successful in life? Why am I not focusing on consciousness continuously, 24 hours a day, as though it was my job, as though I was a teacher or something like that.

People who do astrology say. "This is in your chart, and that is in your chart." I look at them and realize I have no contact with that at all. The chart is not my chart, or it's off by a couple years, or something like that. For a long time it was confusing to me, and in a sense, it's still a little bit confusing,

A part of me knows that basically all I am supposed to do is witness, but a part of me, in this society, is saying, "Why aren't you more successful and ambitious? And if you are not going to be more ambitious in the outward world, why aren't you being successful in the inward world? Be successful someplace. Do not sit there and be." So, there is still that little rub. I know better because this time is like an instant, a flash in existence, but for us it's so concrete that it takes forever. I am not sure how to resolve that. I know on a conscious level it does not make any sense, but I know on this deeper level that it has everything to do with something I need to do, and I am not sure how to resolve that.

S: Would you like me to ask that as a question during the session?

GR: You could ask what is my lesson plan. I know that does not make any sense, because lesson plans are for this concrete reality. Therefore, you understand this concrete reality, and hopefully you get some wisdom about what is or is not. I understand that lesson plans are for this reality. I know there are other realities because I live them by experiencing them, but I do not have the technical language for it. I know in a sense what is and is not real, that what is real is here on earth, and what is real is up there also. But as far as an individual motivating focus, I really do not have that. Part of me seems to want that for some reason. It really does want that.

That is one reason why I never went into the tradition with the Maharishi. I did not pursue the advanced classes, get silent, learn about higher consciousness and transcendence. Part of me does not want to do that. Another part of me does want to do that, but does not want to focus there. Part of me is a cave dweller because he does not want to be successful in this reality. He does not want to be focused. He does not want to be attached to it. It's almost like being schizophrenic in some way. I am being pulled both ways, and I have never really found the happy medium in between where I can do that.

S: Well, there is so much we have been programmed into thinking about what we're supposed to be in this world. It creates a huge conflict all the time.

GR: I tried when I was younger. My focus was on becoming a scientist. But after I learned meditation, I realized there is a whole other realm of experience that is just as wonderful. Part of me wants that. The other part learned computer programming and stuff that is very logical, so you have to figure out routines. Part of me said that what I most enjoy doing is working with my hands. I was a baker for 18 years because I found out I could do stuff with my hands. I could be creative and really enjoy the products I made, and I could see other people enjoying it. Now that I look back on it, that is not really a healthy life cycle for a lot of people. It gives and takes. I guess what I am saying is that I never really found the joy point, the balance between both worlds. I guess it's kind of hard because this world requires a lot of things you have to do. In the celestial realm there is nothing you have to do but be quiet and experience. Daren and I have done a lot of stuff in that sense, re-patterning, doing a process to rewrite our lesson plan, but none of it really worked. She said, "You have to really focus on the exercises." Part of me was saying, "This is not going to do anything for me, so what is the point?"

S: Right.

GR: There is always that little bit of confusion.

S: Yeah. I love an Internet radio show on Sunday mornings called New Dimensions Radio [http://newdimensions.org]. There is this opening statement they always say, that we are not going to solve problems from our intellect, that there has to be a shift in consciousness. That shift in consciousness takes us out of listening to all those people saying, "You have to be smart. You have to make money. You have to be thin. You have to be fat." That was one of the funniest things I noticed when I was in the Peace Corps in Malaysia. Being fat there showed you were prosperous. In Hollywood, skinny is better. How silly all of it is. But to get outside all those limiting or small viewpoints, to be in that big space as you walk through the world cooking, doing the shopping or talking with anybody, and being present with it all, that is so beautiful. It's wonderful, and I seek that out every day.

GR: Part of me wants to be in that reality where we can resolve problems we have on this level of existence, but it does not necessarily require capital or other people's decisions to do things a certain way. I am sure there is a way we can complete our projects, if we want to call them that, the projects in this reality, without going through all the drudgery we have to go through now. I think that is where a level of consciousness raising energy is helping us to get there. But we are not there yet, so I cannot play with those tools yet.

S: I wonder how long it will be before it all gets in place. I can feel daily differences in my own body. There is a humming going on, or it's changing. All I can do is say, "Thank you, thank you, thank you." Sometimes it hurts a bit. It's like turning up the electricity.

GR: I have asked that question about where we need to be. All the explanations I keep getting are, well, it's not time yet. It's close but not time yet. I am tired of hearing that.

S: Right. It's been 30 years that I have been on this path.

GR: It may not be time yet, but is there something we can do now that will express that ability in the future? Because the way we have been brought up, if we are going to do X Y and Z, we need skills X, Y, and Z, so we go to school, so when the time comes to do X, Y, and Z, we can use the skills efficiently. There must be a way of learning what skills we need right now, so that around the corner we could use it.

S: So, you want to ask during the session about what can we do now to realize the manifestation of what we are being shown?

GR: Yeah, but that is a little bit too general. I was hoping for something a little more specific about what things we can do.

S: Show us what we can do.

GR: Yeah. Right now. Here and now. Not what is in the future. Okay, so are we ready to start?

S: Sure. Let's go for it. Let's see what the higher self has for us today.

Session 5: The Importance of Groups

S: Now the cloud is slowing down, and it's stopping at the most appropriate time and place. Now I want you to drift off of that cloud back down, down, down to the surface. There won't be anything sudden. It's like a leaf drifting gently out of a tree, back down to the surface. As you come back down to the surface, I want you to tell me the first thing that you see or the very first impression that you have.

GHS: I am flying over what looks like seacoast, and we come to a hilly area over the green seacoast. It has a village or town of some kind that looks rather primitive, but we land there. My Guide is with me. I am asking him, "Why this place?" It does not look very advanced. He says that because it's a community, it's not necessary to do everything by yourself. It has a group function, not an individual one. He says this place has always been a university, a community working together. It's unnecessary for you to have an individual goal to complete the task at hand. It's a group effort. My Guide says this is where I am most happy -- in the community.

S: So, with this particular group of people, what are you doing together?

GHS: He says the object of being in the community is to participate, to be part of it. It may not look like you are doing a specific thing, but willing participation is a key part of creating what needs to come. An individual can go and be productive, but a person also can be more productive in a community. Being part of the community is what the process is about, not necessarily doing something, but being part of the community.

S: When you are part of the group, and you are gardening or cooking or sewing or listening to music, it's all good.

GHS: Right. It's part of the connection of the individual to the group. The group awareness brings in clearer consciousness, brings in greater contact with what is to be. It's a group effort.

S: Are any of the people in this community in Grapo's present life?

GHS: We are all connected, one way or another. Even when people seem to be strangers, we are all connected. This web of community prepares the way for what is to come next. It's not a matter of technology. In today's society, we have a tendency to isolate ourselves. Isolation disconnects people from each other, even though we stand right next to someone. If an individual goes to a play, whether he goes as an individual or with a friend, during the play he is part of a group called *the audience*. A group consciousness creates another level of reality. There is a time to disconnect, but there is more time that you need to connect with the group. You do not have to know them all individually. Being together as a group is enough.

Consciousness is about being aware of your individual reality. It's also about being aware of your group consciousness. One is not more important than the other. We start as an individual, but we must leave our homes and become part of a community. This is the way forward.

We have isolated ourselves too much. The potter creates the pots, but it becomes an extra value when the potter takes his pot to the group. All may be aware of its function, its beauty, but the process is not complete because it's a visual we create. It must be shared. You cannot do that by yourself. That is done in the community, whether you are shopping or exploring. We must go out and be part of a community. Only when we think that we are by ourselves do we think we are not accomplishing anything? You would be surprised how much you can accomplish when you go to a movie because we connect there with the group. There we share our thoughts; we share our activities. We become isolated only when we stop sharing.

We have difficulty seeing what is to come when we are not in a group. This process seems to be from the outside, an individual process, but it's not. All around the world, others are participating. We are doing this in a group manner, in the group awareness. Even children go to the mall to hang out together. They are expressing the need for group consciousness. The smallest stroke of activity creates greater levels of activity when we are in a group.

S: Is Grapo having enough opportunity to be in groups with what he's engaged in?

GHS: On a higher conscious level, he is. But his disconnect with this world is his lack of activity with others.

S: From what I know of him, he and his family live in a family compound. He has his medical support at this time because he's going through a great deal of intense care for his body. Are you suggesting that there could be other things he could do that would enhance his energy and the energy of the group?

GHS: He has always been searching. He has never stopped. He has always been seeking clarity on what to do. He has not found it yet. But the process cannot be found unless he is active within a larger group. We all gain greater clarity when we are actively in the world. We can create joy. We can create objects. The greater value, the greater consciousness, is brought about by bringing it into the community. As individuals you can express different levels of consciousness. If this art is taken into the community, its greater value will be expressed. The process will be complete. Creations are not the activities that matters. What matters is not the act itself but sharing with the group. The full stroke of consciousness is from the individual into the group consciousness. It does not stop at the individual level. It's not complete if it's held by the individual. This is not to say that being alone and being creative is not productive. It is. But that productivity is not complete until it's shared.

S: I feel like you are talking to me more than you are talking to Grapo right now.

GHS: This is a universal principle. It happens with everyone. It is the *First Principle*. It is the movement from individual outward. It is the movement from group consciousness to singularity. The process is complete both ways. When we flow in the stream of life and flow towards the Source, the coalescing out of the stream into this consciousness, into this realm, is a one-stroke process. When we flow from this level of conscious-ness, it's a group consciousness, a group activity. We flow into another stroke of that process. That stroke creates the process to bring us to the next level of consciousness and our eventual return to the stream of life. When we create and gain wisdom for ourselves, that is one process, one stroke of activity. When we leave the ranch and travel into group consciousness, that is another stroke.

Group consciousness leads to another level of awareness, and that is the creative process, which wishes to emerge. That is the en-gine of our progress. That is why it's said that no man is an island. When we put on our shields and protect ourselves and do what we feel we need to do, this is an act of getting behind the brake to slow things down. When we take what we have learned, and we share it with others, this is releasing the brake, and so we flow to greater consciousness. When we travel to different places, this is the process of releasing the brakes. We are moving the choices. This is the process of traveling to create greater consciousness. It's not required for us to do both. Humanity feels lost, mostly when it thinks by itself and acts by itself. Greater clarity is achieved in-group consciousness.

S: I get the impression that two or three people could be a group. There is something that happens there as well as larger groups. But the group can be anything, as you said, whether going to a movie or going shopping.

GHS: Yes.

S: It connects us to go to the coffee shop and share that space with others. And when we do something with that connection, then maybe we will consciously recognize it.

GHS: Yes.

S: And it's good to be with others.

GHS: Whether you are aware of it or not, moving into a group creates connections even if you are not consciously aware of it.

S: Yes. I think you have given quite a good answer to something we were discussing before we started this session, about what we can do now. Is there anything else you can add to that? What can we do now, so that where we are going and what is coming for us is more a joy point for Grapo?

GHS: It does not only bring us clarity and joy. It brings us healing, as well.

S: I know there are different levels of healing. There is the physical, which Grapo is dealing with in his current life, and emotional issues, as with friends, plus a spiritual level, and mental level of accomplishments. One of the things that Grapo wanted is clarification on how much he is influenced by things other people tell him he should be doing, ought to be doing, ought to be thinking or believing. How much can he do now within a group, now that he's able to sort out what is true for him. How is he doing on that?

GHS: It's part of the process. Greater levels of group consciousness bring greater levels of discernment. Thoughts of healing bring goodwill that you will find in a group. That is the intimate creation in this world. Again, the individual process is complete when it's done in a group.

S: Is Grapo in a frame of mind where he is able to allow more group activity in his life now?

GHS: Yes.

S: Of course, you are always there with him. Will you be assisting him in choosing the group or groups to participate in that will bring out the highest expression of him?

GHS: It's his choice.

S: Is that the choice he's making?

GHS: Yes.

S: Okay. Good. Now, are he and I getting together here an expression of group?

GHS: Yes.

S: I look forward to it very much. I feel the energy enhancing both of us. Thank you for being with us in this way. I know we have not expressed this exactly right, but Grapo would like a more consistent knowing or feeling of being in presence with you as his Guide, in all of his daily activities. Has that been increasing as we have been getting together?

GHS: Yes. The clarity has been helpful in that process.

S: Right now I am seeing waves, like the pebble in the pond. That is the clarity coming to him and me. It's radiating out in our fields wherever we go in the day, to some extent. Is that true?

GHS: Yes. It's also important to be physically present in larger groups. Otherwise, the process is not complete.

S: I see.

GHS: We have a physical connection in this world, and it's the proximity to one another that brings greater consciousness. The cave dweller has individual consciousness, expresses his higher level of consciousness in isolation; but the process is not complete unless he walks among other people. It's not necessary for him to share who he is. His mere presence in the group of people increases that value of consciousness. We are moving away from thinking of ourselves as individuals. The individual consciousness, individual awareness is expanding. It's important that this is happening not only on the conscious level but also on the physical level. Humanity needs to learn that the process is accelerated when we do it as a group, and it's physical proximity is important. Consciousness pervades everything. But the physical process is also very important.

Be at peace.

S: Thank you. Thank you so much for being with us today and for clarifying the connection, the greater connection for both of us.

Session Debrief

GR: As individuals, we realize through raising our level of consciousness, thereby becoming aware of different levels of consciousness, that there exists a greater whole. If you take that lesson and apply it on a physical level to one individual at any level of consciousness, and if you put him in a group, the level of individual consciousness is raised, even though he or she did not meditate. The sheer physical presence of individuals being closer and closer together raises the level of consciousness. Getting together as a group increases level of discernment for all individuals in that group.

So, when you send campaign letters to individuals or you send emails to individuals through the internet, that is not as powerful as getting all those individuals together in one room. A monk who sits alone raises consciousness, but physically getting together raises consciousness, too. You bring your value to the group. You do not have to bring a message. You do not have to bring your wisdom. It's physically being present that is most important.

Your level of consciousness is a magnetic field. As you increase your level of consciousness, the strength of that field increases. When you walk into a group of individuals, at that point you share a higher level of intensity. They do not necessarily have to be aware of it, but their processes are amplified. If we all go into caves and do our process, that is one half of the coin. That individual has to move out into society. Whether we teach or do not teach, that value of raised consciousness and wisdom is being shared, whether we are aware of it or not.

This is basically the driving force behind why we do not stay in small villages. We keep gathering and gathering and gathering in bigger and bigger and bigger populations because that is the actual process of going from a primitive society to an advanced society. Now we are at this time and space where we are getting together individual consciousness and raising it by many individuals. So, when we get together as a group in a bigger society, that process brings about the change. That exponential ability is what is helping to bring a greater level of consciousness to the world, not necessarily just to the individual.

We tend to focus on our own process. Well, what is my purpose, or what is your purpose, or what is Daren's purpose? We are doing what we need to do, but the important thing here is that we must take what we are doing, whether consciously or not, going out into a society or not, and we have to get physical proximity to a group.

That is important, very important, because as individuals, we are like magnets. We only exert a certain amount of influence over our environment. It's when we get together in closer proximity, like when we go to a movie, that we share that level of consciousness. Although we are sharing the movie, we are sharing a great deal more than that. What is really necessary is for us to get out, to go out.

We are people of the ground. We are people of the earth. When we travel to other places and open up our consciousness, what we are doing is sharing it with other people. That is the outward stroke. That is the process of developing the new consciousness, the new world that we are all seeking. To sit in our own individual level of comfort is not doing that process. That is why we are constantly driven to do something else. That is why our interest is taken to other places. I may not be a great artist, but if I go to a gallery and other people are there, then I am sharing that value of wisdom and that value of consciousness on an another level all together.

This is why we have that drive to go places. That is an actual mechanism by which we are driving ourselves into higher level of consciousness. We keep hoping for The New Age to arrive, to come *to* us. In reality, it is coming *through* us because we are reaching others as individuals. We are creating a bigger and bigger battery, so to speak. The physical process is extremely important. We have tended to over emphasize our individual process, and we have lost our perspective that way. It's as important to walk outside, go to the basketball game or go to the movie or go to the mall, because there are more and more people there physically. That stroke of physically getting closer to individuals is also the value of consciousness that is being raised. Whether you are aware of it or not, like I said, does not matter.

S: Isn't that great?

GR: Yeah. And that is the clarity that I was asking about, the individual process. Whenever we look at ourselves, we turn inward and ask, "What do I need to do?" The answer is that you need to do what you feel, what you discern is important in the level of consciousness. But what you really need to do also is complete the process.

The value of consciousness is shared at the group level. So, if your desire or your discernment is to create a new society, you are sharing that with that group consciousness, and that group consciousness is now bringing in that new world, that new understanding, that greater clarity.

Humanity tends to think of themselves as individuals first. When we create in our own world what we think is real, we go out into society and expand our consciousness, whatever level it is, and we share that reality. So, if our reality is that we are capitalists, and we think this way because of our religious teachings, we go out into the world and create that reality. Not create that reality as much as share that reality. That is why it's important, as an individual, that you come to some level of conscious awareness of what is the whole process. You have to get some level of clarity. That level of clarity, that level of peace and harmony and understanding, is what you will share in the group.

If you go into another group that does not have those particular values, you are helping to enlighten them. You are helping to expand their consciousness, expand their awareness. There may be friction because those individuals do not want to change. They think their reality is what consciousness is all about.

The greater the group consciousness becomes, there is greater harmony, and greater consciousness. We as individuals are bringing in that level of consciousness. The people in that other group, as hard as they may want to resist, are slowly changing their minds, slowly changing their level of understanding. That is why the physical proximity is very important. We are charging ourselves as super batteries, and when we walk into a group, we help every other physical individual there.

I think the New Age focus on the development of individual self-awareness needs to be balanced with collective group awareness. We are becoming more consciously aware as individuals, but the Guides are saying that it's equally important that we physically step away from being alone and towards being together with others in groups. That is part of the process of the First Principle. The First Principle is always moving forward. If we bring our level of awareness to another individual physically who does not understand it, they move forward also. Even if they put on the brakes, we are helping them move forward. If it's one individual, we have one value. If it's two individuals, we have two values. If we have one individual who is not moving fast, and we have 20 individuals who are moving fast, if they are physically in the same spot, the slower individual begins moving forward a lot faster than he was originally.

The march to the capital building of individuals to express their opinions is actually not an intellectual process. They are bringing a physical conscious awareness. All these individuals in the Middle East did not spontaneously get up and decide to have the "Arab Spring" uprising. It was getting together as a group that raised everyone's consciousness, and that is the process that snowballed. But in the process you had other individuals who did not want to change, and they tried to stop that consciousness raising effect.

War is not about bringing people together. It's about separating them. Individuals again. War lowers everybody's group consciousness. It makes them less effective. This is why dictators do not want people to gather. They do not want the Chinese to gather in the square. They do not want Muslims to gather in a park. Our society does not want us to gather together in rallies. It's because those individuals who do not want to change, without intellectually understanding it, know that if we are physically brought together, we can express a higher consciousness than the individuals can alone. We will be much harder to control and eventually we will develop group self-control, through a process similar to how, as individuals, we developed self-control.

So, actually, we are doing the process. My question is, what should *I* do? The answer is simply that I have done the one process of being an individual focused on consciousness raising for myself. Now my process is to walk out into the mall, out into the community. My frustration comes about because I cannot easily get out like I used to. That is where I get frustrated. Being together with my brothers and sisters and family is one level of helping to raise consciousness. I do not talk too much with my brother and sister about this process that is going on, but I know intuitively they have a greater level of awareness because, from time to time, they ask a question without being direct.

S: Yes.

GR: So, the whole process is continuing on the family level, but the process must continue on the whole group level. Not just as a village, not just as a town, not just as a city, (those are the beginnings) but eventually as a nation, and finally, as a world whole.

S: As the whole world, and then eventually all that is, everything.

GR: Right. And that is why it's important for us as individuals to gather together in groups and do any activity. Physical cooperation is as important as the individual process. It's part of the American society that values — because this is the way we thought of ourselves and how our ancestors thought of themselves — that when we came to America, we wanted to be able to express our individuality while simultaneously NOT being driven by select groups of *others*.

S: We had to do individual development first.

G: Right. And the focus now is almost fully set as in concrete, that the individual is the center core of American society. If you want to make it in America, you can. You have the potential. You have the choices. You have the resources. But that really is not true. Some people have all they need for success, but not everybody has it.

And what the Guides were saying to me, as I understand it, was that in order for us to grow as a whole, and we are growing, we must change our way of thinking a bit. The individual is the first step, the one stroke. The other stroke is the process of us getting together and helping everybody else.

That is why the First Principle applies here, also, because it's always a forward movement. It's always a stroke towards the Source, whether we like it or not. No matter how hard we make a choice to set the brakes, we are still moving in that direction.

We ask ourselves, how can we move faster? How can we accelerate the process? How can we make that higher consciousness happen now? It's a very simple process. You go into a larger group. To travel, you leave Home. This is a way of saying, stop living as an individual and move into society. That is the value that increases the whole of society, the value that changes everything. The point is that even the physical presence changes the consciousness. In a way, individual consciousness raises the individual, physical proximity in a group of individuals raises the oneness of everyone in the group.

S: Is this exponential?

GR: Exponential consciousness, so everybody experiences it, whether they are at the level of awareness or not.

S: Beautiful.

GR: The First Principle still applies. I think that is why the Guides touched on the First Principle process in our very first session. It's actually the process that we are going through right now. It's the process we need to continue to focus upon and follow on a physical level. We are always saying, what can we do physically to make the change in the world? Could I create a new engine? Can I create a new piece of art? Yes, you can, but what you need to do is take your individual self and place yourself in the community. That very process brings about the change.

It came across in my understanding we need the other half of the coin, that the coin is not complete unless you have both halves. That point that kept slapping me over and over and over when I was listening to the session recording. It's very important. It's one thing to have art in your home. It's another thing if you put that art on display in society. Whether they want to see it or not is irrelevant; the value of you being there with your art raises everybody's individual consciousness, whether they come and say, "Oh, I like your art," or they look briefly and walk on. They do not realize that you are creating a value for them of raising their conscious awareness.

So the question is: How do we bring about the New Age? We are doing that by stepping outside of our individual roles and stepping into the community. We just have to get together and talk about this. If we bring to society our awareness of what we think we should do, then that will fulfill the requirements for the coming of the changes. What we need to remember is that if I individually walk into a group as a total stranger, that raises their value, too. The whole process is complete, whether we are focusing on it or not.

This is why some of the Guides say, "It is coming, and you cannot stop it." It's a joke, a personal joke, because they understand that "what is coming" is that we are doing what we need to do. It's coming because we are bringing it about. We are bringing it into fruition. The Guides are helping with the energies, but *we* are bringing it into fruition. It's also important that we get together and do it physically, whether on purpose or not.

S: I get it. I cannot find an analogy right now, but I do understand it.

GR: So if I leave here today and I go to downtown Lihue, and I walk into Subway and have a sandwich, that is actually part of the process of raising consciousness.

S: Right. Isn't that wonderful, we can just do what we do?

GR: I do not even have to go in there and talk to anybody about it.

S: It's your energy field. Energy gets transmitted. It gets collected. It gets shared and exchanged. I think that is one of the reasons the message has been coming down about how important it's to hug. Hugging is an exchange. When you hug somebody that is more than you can do yourself.

GR: And we do it whether you know it or not. We cannot avoid the process. It's going to go on. It's continuous, that is where the First Principle is expressed over and over in our actions. I think part of the reason the Guidance brought out the First Principle is to bring in greater and greater clarity. So many people have questions about the process. That process is what the Guides are bringing to us. If we have clarity in the process, then we act naturally and do things in a way the process is supposed to occur. We do not have to create a new religion. We do not have to create a new society. All we have to do is bring that process into our awareness and physically walk outside into society. That brings about the change.

So, I think that is the New Age answer. We no longer have to question anymore what the process is. The Guides are bringing that clarity to us. They are bringing it into our awareness. We do not have to confuse ourselves by trying to figure it out for ourselves.

S: The mind has not done a very good job?

GR: It's constantly probing.

S: Entertainment value.

GR: This session has really helped me a lot.

S: Good. Me too. Yeah, we have done a good sharing here?

GR: Which is probably why they said we have to do a book.

S: Yeah. It is a way for us to...

GR: Share with them. Society.

S: Yes. Yes.

GR: If we can share it with X amount of people, they share it with somebody else. Even if it's not at every moment in their conscious awareness, when they get together and go shopping or to the mall, whatever they do in their daily activities with other people, they are sharing it, whether they are aware of it or not. That is the important second half of the coin. We understand the first half because we have spent the last hundreds of years trying to figure it out, but the obvious second half was harder to see, because when you are in the midst of a crowd, it's hard to determine what the rest of the crowd is doing. You do not necessarily have conscious understanding of what they are doing, that is the key. I hope this part of the message gets out to everybody. Then we will stop asking, "When is the New Age going to happen?"

S: It is happening now. We are doing it right now.

CHAPTER 7

BURNING WORLDS THAT DO
NOT BURN THE SOUL

*G*rapo was greatly excited about this session. It seems to be a key to everything else in this unfolding story of Creation and beyond. In his excitement, he went home and transcribed this session on his own. I've used his telling of the session instead of the regular transcriptions. You will notice the difference in the style for this write up. It's more lively, as he is telling the story, not only as it came on the taped recording, but from his own view.

In this session is a reference to Jesus. Grapo and I have talked about this, thinking that we need to say something about it. So, I am offering this preface.

Grapo has spent one past life, that we know about, as a monk. In this life, Grapo relates to Jesus, not as we know him in our religions, but as a teacher and brother.

Grapo was brought up in this life as a Catholic. He moved away from the Church's representation of Christ sometime in his late teens. It was soon after that he became a Transcendental Meditator (TM) He also studied to be a Reiki Master.

He has experienced his abilities to transcend the commonly agreed-upon reality of our world by connecting with his subconscious in these Quantum Healing Hypnosis Therapy sessions. It's clear throughout these materials

87

that everyone has their own spiritual path. The Divine comes to each one as the one to whom they are most closely connected. When you connect to your Divine, what or whom do you see? For Grapo, it is Jesus.

Session 6: Fire Worlds

GR: I have come off the cloud and see an old world village made of stone. I am an old male wearing sandals. My clothing is plain and peasant-like, old and tattered. My skin is old and very wrinkled, dark brown in color. I am not wearing jewelry of any kind, but I am wearing a simple hat.

The town is an image of two superimposed images. One is Old World stucco. Overlaying this is an image of what looks to be volcanic activity of fire and lava hot spots with a general feeling of heat. There is no smoke of any kind in the vision.

I see one other person beside myself, an older lady. I do not know her name. She is round and short in body, as old and wrinkled as myself. I am filled with affection for her. Speaking from higher consciousness, "we" call her "Sister."

She looks at me and says, "We are a long way from Home. We are from a world where our task is to travel and learn."

At this time I had no clear understanding of my home world. We have met in many different worlds other than Earth or our home world. She is acting as my Guide at this point to make clear my journey in this time and place called Earth. Sister is older than I am and a great deal more experienced than I am -- even though I have been a traveler for many centuries. In point of fact, I was her student in the beginning of my travels.

She calls me by name, "Grapo," which means "of the land," a traveler of many different lands. She stands there considering my history and my purpose for this engagement. She conveys the image of the land around me being on fire, emphasizing the importance of the image. It's a fire unlike any other type of fire we are accustomed to seeing. She says that this is the "Fire that does not burn the Soul." She says this "Fire" portrays a sense of immortality.

She said I see in my understanding that this is a world of rocks and water, but Earth's true nature is one of Fire. This Fire does not burn the land or evaporate the water, and does not burn the Soul. This Fire is not the fire we cook with. It's deep red in color and never burns the soul. It's the essence and foundation of this world. This Fire cannot be seen or felt from a normal perspective, but it does make people jumpy. Sister says it's a cleansing fire. We perceive this world as a blue green world of flowing water, but when seen from a higher consciousness, it's a world in flames of Fire.

At this point I am overwhelmed by the energy of this knowledge as I become aware of what this Fire truly means. For this Fire is the Love of God. As God's love flows through me, I am unable to speak for a time.

I finally ask Sister why is the Earth a world of Fire? She says it's because its basic constituents cannot be broken down any further. It's a pure element. Mankind needs to know this because it's the truth of this world. This Fire is the energy that maintains the world we see. As consciousness flows through our mind and our body, so does Fire flow through Gaia and us. As we learn of our wholeness in consciousness, Gaia learns of the created worlds through Fire. Fire is the kin to the light of consciousness of Gaia, and she learns of the Burning Worlds through Fire. As we are birthed from the Living Light, Gaia is birthed from the expression of God through this eternal Fire.

We share a connection with Gaia and our selves. We shine through the Living Light, and Gaia shines through the consciousness of the living God through Fire. As Gaia burns brighter, so does the consciousness of mankind burn brighter. Mankind cannot avoid this even if there are those who do not want to express Gaia's burning Love. Mankind cannot escape or avoid this process.

There are those who do not seek to express Gaia's burning love, but they cannot resist this because mankind walks hand in hand with Gaia's evolution.

I ask Sister, "Has this anything to do with global warming?"

Sister replies, "Yes, and in a greater sense, No. Global warming is the thinnest outer shell of Gaia's potential. The melting of polar ice is a part of the transition for Gaia. The changes in the environment and the atmosphere are an expression of the change in Gaia's higher consciousness through Fire. It's part of Gaia's and mankind's evolving consciousness through this time of transition, and it should not be mankind's point of focus."

From mankind's perspective, the seeds of karma are consumed in the fire of higher consciousness, so it's removed from mankind. This process is reflected in Gaia by the Fire, causing changes in what we see as global changes. This is Gaia expressing the will of the Living Light of God. As we learn through consciousness to return to the Living Light, so Gaia through her evolution returns to the Living Light of God and Source. This world may be of water, but Gaia burns with the Living Light of Fire. Gaia is consumed by Fire as the sun is consumed by fire, but unlike the sun, Gaia's Fire does not burn the Soul.

I am told that Sister and I have traveled to many worlds, and these worlds all burn with the Fire as its elemental source. A network of Burning Worlds on the solar level is the purity of this world. It is, in effect, a network of Burning Worlds in which Gaia and mankind travel to higher consciousness and into a more evolved physical world expressing new laws of both consciousness and physics.

People see Gaia as a green world, but higher self sees her as the heart of a burning red rose, a world on fire, burning in brilliance, and it's this gift she shares with humanity. This energy is influencing mankind's compassion to help mankind to change. It's not consciousness alone that causes us to change. As we are immortal in the stream of light and in Source, the Fire Worlds, the Burning Worlds, are eternal in their own way in the physical universe.

The two processes, consciousness and Fire, cannot be disengaged from each other, for one effects the other. As in the beginning we are birthed in the stream of light through consciousness, so this is reflected in the physical earth through the burning Fire as its basic element. As we flow through the stream of light, the Burning Worlds flow through the stream of Fire in the physical universe.

There are other worlds that flow in a stream other than Fire, in another element of their own, but earth flows in a network of worlds in a stream of fire that burns eternally and does not burn the Soul. We are able to walk the earth because this Fire does not burn the Soul.

I ask Sister why does our sun burn the soul? How does our sun not burn us to the point that the soul is disfigured or destroyed, as we understand it?

Sister tells me that when considering my attachment to this world, I must see it through this element of Fire. When each of us is considering Self in consciousness, we must consider it in the light of the Living Light the Living God. That Living Fire is the expression in the physical world of the Living God. Earth is a Fire World. As we touch the grass, as we breathe the air, as we see the beauty of this world, it's through the basic element of burning fire. It's through our consciousness that we see the blues, the yellows, and the beauty of this world as an expression of the element of earth's own source, which is Fire. Beautiful light of fire.

Humanity benefits from the network of Burning Worlds, the Fire Worlds. Humanity travels hand in hand within the network of Fire Worlds. Within the network of Fire Worlds, humanity exists in this universe; it's part of humanity's expression. As our consciousness evolves, as the earth grows through the burning fire in the Living Love, or the Living God's Fire, we will come to understand the network of Burning Worlds. The network of humanity will come to appreciate their expression in the physical world.

Humanity expresses itself as the coalescence of the Living Stream of Light into consciousness and into the network of Burning Fire Worlds. There are other worlds flowing from other forms of energy. Mankind flows into the Fire World networks as they travel throughout the universe. Mankind walks upon the Fire Worlds as you would walk across a stream on stones in that stream. This is our connection in the physical universe.

This also is the Truth of the First Principle. We may through consciousness travel through different worlds, different lives, but they are all being expressed through the Fire World network. This is not by chance. This is on purpose.

The Living Stream of Light is like the left hand of evolution, and the right hand is the Burning Worlds of Fire, of physical evolution. We move as one.

There is an image being shown to me. It's the image of Jesus with both palms up toward God. What we see is Creation. What we see is the unfolding of the Stream of Living Light. We see the unfolding of conscious beings from the Living Light Stream into the Burning Worlds of Fire of the Living God.

As we desire to return to the Source through the Living Light Stream, humanity's physical existence desires to travel through the network of Fire Worlds. These worlds may be different from our perspective, each colored by our level of consciousness, but they are humanity's Burning Worlds. This is why our beloved Jesus stands before you with open hands. He is representing humanity's path, returning to the Living Light of Source, and the physical expressions of God's Burning World network we travel within. This is the knowledge that was brought forth and given to mankind by the Christ Consciousness. You may experience different worlds and experience other lives, but all belong to the network of Burning Worlds. This is the gift of God in the physical universe.

So, as we travel through the Living Light to Source we are also at the same time traveling through the physical network of Burning Worlds that is the gift of God's Light and Love.

At this point, Grapo transmits a message directly from the Guides

G: We hope this message brings some level of clarity to yourself and all of humanity. When humanity wants to ask what is next, understand that you have been given a gift by God to travel through the network of Fire Worlds. What comes next for you has already been given to you by and through the love of God in this physical universe. God awaits us all in the new world that burns with the light which does not burn souls, for which humanity yearns. This will be your new home! It's the gift of Christ Consciousness to know and understand this clearly. You must understand this not only in the light of consciousness but also on the level of compassion in your heart. Envision a loving Christ before you with both hands up. This is his teaching and gift to each of you.

This is why we express the First Principle, which is always flowing nonstop in the stream of life. The element of Fire is the living love of God's consciousness giving rise to this world. This is what Gaia desires and flows toward and through. This is what humanity flows toward and through with Gaia. There is no stopping this flow. It flows, and no one can stop it! Not other beings, not others' wills. This is the gift we give to you that expresses the First Principle. It expresses the will of God that expresses the will of the Living Light and the Source.

Yes, there is more for humanity at the end where we meet the Source, even at the end of the network of Burning Worlds that do not burn souls, but this is your journey. This is mankind's journey, one world at a time. Whatever level of consciousness you travel, it's one world at a time, and we are here to see that you travel. We will help you in every day, in every way in every effort. This process cannot be stopped! We are Guides. We come to you to bring clarity, to bring understanding, not only on the level of consciousness

but also on the level of the heart, so intellect can understand and experience what is happening to you and your world.

We bring you peace and the love of the everlasting God through the Burning Worlds that do not burn souls.

Be at peace.

After the session, Grapo and I do a debrief to discuss the material that came through. Here is a transcript of that conversation.

GR: Oh my gosh! It never stops.

S: That was wonderful! Fantastic. What energy was present with us today? Golly!

GR: It seems very important we know this. Fire is earth's basic element. Our basic element is consciousness. Earth's basic element is the Fire that does not burn souls.

When we were having that vision, and we were traveling to the place where I ended up seeing this village -- the architecture looked kind of like a Pueblo Indian village -- the place was on fire at first. It was like lava, volcanic. It reminded me of the Vulcan world on Star Trek.

It was confusing because I kept asking if I could see my Guide consciously while you were talking, or if I could have an image of who is my Guide. I said I'd like to see my Guide in a form at whatever level I could understand, and then Sister appeared. She was an older lady, like an ancient Pueblo woman. She was not very tall, kind of round. She wore a shawl around her shoulders. Her dress was very simple.

She smiled at me and said, "I am a great deal older than I look."

I said, "Well, I am confused because I see this world is burning." The only thought that came to me as I was talking to her was that the Gita says, "Sit in silence and burn the seeds of karma." In other words, burn the seeds of action.

I asked how all this related to what I was seeing, and then the whole image changed. I saw the world as we'd see it from space. A beautiful world of swirling blues and greens.

She said, "That is what you see through your physical eyes. Look through Gaia's eyes." Then the world was there, but it was this brilliant dark red of burning flames. I could not understand.

This is the basic element of Gaia, she said. If you see yourself as consciousness and your identity as soul, this is how Gaia sees herself, as the burning flame.

I saw flames all over the place. At first I was confused. I asked, "If we are living here, how come we are not burning up?

That was when she said, "This is the Living Light of God's love. It's the burning Flame that does not burn souls."

That image was the clarity she was giving us. It came into my mind because I was confused. She was talking about the physical evolution and the universe and at the same time as she was showing us our conscious spiritual evolution.

This is given to us through the Christ Consciousness. The image in my mind popped up as the image of Christ standing before me with both hands out and down at his sides. Then they said, "This is what the Christ Consciousness meant. It's the revelation that God exists in the universe as burning love in this physical world."

We think we can go to the moon, or someday we will travel in outer space to other worlds. Humanity is traveling, but not to different environments as we consciously or physically see it. Humanity is traveling into different Fire Worlds that have the Living Light of God in them. That is God's gift.

We are traveling to these worlds in different levels of consciousness. As we travel, we see the world through our physical eyes or through whatever level of consciousness we can see. But its basic element is a Fire World. Its basic element is Fire, a very different fire, that is a very dark red. It's not burning like the sun, as we see images of it, which is a yellow burning at different intensities. This is a deep red that is the love of God.

Though we are traveling, evolving in our level of consciousness in the stream of life, the other half of the coin is that we are traveling through different worlds. We may ask, what is our next world going to be like? Our next world is going to be in the network of Burning Fire Worlds that do not burn the souls. We are traveling through God's worlds. We may see something physically different to our physical eyes, but it's another world like this one. So, this answers our question about what is next.

The answer is another world where our consciousness is more evolved, where our connection with our heart is more open to all that love that God has given us. I cannot picture the next world, but they are giving us a clarity of understanding about what we are going through right now. It almost makes the question about the next world meaningless because it's going to be as beautiful and as loving as the world we *want* now.

I never would have thought there was a dual process going on. It's interesting. The whole time they kept expressing that the earth is a Burning World. Even though we see it from space as a water world, it's a Burning World. On the side, I grasped an understanding that there are other worlds, like water worlds, or Gem Worlds that have different elements to them. It's a network of worlds to which other people are traveling. I do not know how to put it. Those worlds are not humanity's path. The Burning Worlds are humanity's path.

When we do consciousness traveling, we see all these different worlds. Like the one I visited originally, where it was very calm, and it had the pink trees and a magenta sky. I see that in one sense as a different world. They are saying it's another Burning World of Fire. The elemental Fire of God, the source of love.

No matter what we see, it's another world being expressed through the love of God. We do not see it that way because we do not see it through Gaia's physical existence. We see it through our own consciousness. Gaia is incredible because it's unique. People have said in the universe that Earth is unique. Earth has a spectrum no other planet has. That 's because Earth is a Burning

World, and another world that does not have our beauty, as we see it, is another elemental expression in the physical universe. It's not our world. It's not humanity's world. It's not our path.

This is interesting because I always thought we would be traveling to other worlds in this universe, but that 's not they way it's set up. We are traveling through our worlds, the Fire Worlds.

S: I love it being expressed as a network.

GR: I've seen a streak, worlds after worlds, not all in a line, but all connected like a network. Our evolution is through this network.

This is the path on the physical sense as seen through Gaia, but our consciousness flows through the stream of light [life], from which we are never separated. It seems that we stepped out or co-alesced out of the stream of life [light], but we are not lost because we step onto the network that is parallel to conscious evolution at a soul level of evolution. We are traveling in a physical stream of light. Every time mankind desires something else, that something else is a gift of God through Christ Consciousness. We are traveling the path of the living worlds of the burning light that does not burn souls.

So, in that sense, mankind is never lost. Mankind has not fallen like some angel from the love of god.

S: This is rewriting history.

GR: Very much so. I do not see angels as fallen anymore. I think they have their path, and we have our path. Maybe at times our paths coalesce, but according to my Guide and what she showed me, mankind and humanity are on their own path.

CHAPTER 8

EVOLUTION OF
CONSCIOUSNESS

Discussion Before the Session

*G*rapo is talking about a recent dreaming experience. He wants to understand its meaning for him and its larger significance.

GR: You could call this experience a dream, but I do not call it a dream. You wake up from dreams. You remember them. They are very odd. People say you can lucid dream, and then you can control it. You want to find out what the message means.

I had this dream. I woke up in the middle of it while still being in the dream and I said, "Well this is interesting." I was in a city. I do not know what city. There was some construction work going on, and this young guy in his twenties came up to me. He said," Hey, can you loan me a couple bucks? " He wanted to get somewhere. I said, "no problem," and I went to give him a couple of dollars. I do not know why it was important for me to notice that I had a five-dollar bill, a one-dollar bill, and some changes. He said, "Oh, you have a five." I said, "I cannot give you that because I wouldn't have anything left." So, I gave him a dollar and the change, which came to about two dollars. And he was happy to get that.

Then this other guy walked up. I guess he was listening to what was going on. He was a tall black man, really well dressed. He said, "Hey, you need some help?" I said, "I gave him a couple of dollars, but he has a question. He wants to find a warm place he can stay for the night." The well-dressed man said, "I know a place," and he told me the cross streets. It's not a bus terminal, but a place he can layover, and it's heated. If he wants to stay out of the cold and keep warm, that is where he can go."

I have no clue whatsoever what all this was all about. It seemed like I had nothing to do with what was going on. I turned around and started walking toward a bus stop. This little girl ran up to me. She could not be more than two years old or something like that. This was by a house next to the construction site. There were two elderly women, like grandmas. I walked up to them. This one woman was all happy and smiling. I looked down on the ground, and there was this little cube, glowing a kind of red-dish color. I looked down and said, "That is weird." She looked at me and smiled, like she could see it, too. "You could see that?" I asked. She said, "Yeah, they are all over the place. They are part of the nature of this world." The little girl was really happy. She was playing with a cube. I bent down and tried to reach for this cube. Energy was pouring out of it, like hot air. I could feel it.

I looked around and saw cubes all over place. I could see the energy coming out of the trees and the rocks and stuff. I thought, "This is really unusual," but the kid looked at me, smiled, and said, "No, it's not. This is normal."

That was when I realized this is the next step in earth's evolution. In the next world, energy is free for everybody to use, to see, to touch. Energy is not an issue anymore, like how do we heat our houses, because we all know how to manipulate the organic energies of the planet. The kids take it so naturally and seamlessly.

S: Yes, we are going to use pure energy to create things with our thoughts. And collectively, if we get together, if we have a common intention, it's going to be much easier. There is going to be total cooperation in this, and we are going to play and have fun with it all. When we finish with something, it's going to go back into pure energy form, so we do not have to take care of it all the time, you know, like get insurance for it.

GR: That is a good point.

S: In one of your sessions, your Guide said that in this world, as it is, we eat animals, and it's part of the reality we are in right now, but this reality is going to shift. As we get through to the next Burning World, will we be of a frequency where we don't need to eat food at all? Will we have energy that is free?

G: To me it seems that our evolution in the physical world goes hand in hand with the consciousness of the body. As we consciously evolve, our body has to evolve with it, so whatever world we go to, whatever level of consciousness we are in, all those abilities will be there for us to use. It's a constant evolution in that direction. The hard thing for everybody, I think, is that we are not there; we are here. Yet we have prior knowledge of what is to come, so we want that here now. And even if we do not have full knowledge, or even an intuitive input, somewhere deep down we know there is something better.

S: I do not know if everybody does. We are on a different level in our exploration of this. Like Guidance said, you've been here a really long time. We are far from Home, but we are still curious, and we want to know what is going on. We are exploring. We went way out and came back in. Now we are getting information going a little further in increments from the Guidance. Does that seem right to you?

GR: Yes. We are moving along. We have to be patient.

S: Well, in being so close with you and the information you are bringing through, and then doing my own processing of it, I have seen the importance of enjoying this life. Standing out in the driveway for about 15 minutes earlier today, I was looking at the tree. The cats came and played with each other, having some fun. Then I was watching a bee for a while. All these little vignettes felt so precious and beautiful. I was so peaceful. It was lovely. There was nothing else to do but be in the moment.

GR: Yeah. I think that is the best part of this world myself.

S: Just soak up the sun.

GR: Exactly. Sometimes when I am waiting for my sister, if we are going shopping or something, I stand outside, waiting by the car. I look up to see the sun. I look down at the ground. I see little things to get curious about. It's being in the moment, and enjoying what is there. It's really, really nice. Some people do not see any of that.

S: No. And maybe they do not need to see it. Their path is their path. Let them have it. That is my motto now. Let them have their path, and I'll get on with mine.

GR: So, what do we have in mind for this session?

S: Nothing. We get together, and we find out what happens.

GR: I think so.

S: As you know, I have been getting these sessions transcribed, so we can produce some kind of book to share all this information coming though you.

GR: Yeah. I think we need that. I am the kind of person, and I have a feeling you are the same way, that if I physically read it over and over, look at it, then it becomes clear.

S: Absolutely. I have to do that. I try every possible way to get this information into my life. I read and underline the transcripts. I listen to the recorded sessions in my car. Every time I take off in my car, I turn it on and listen some more.

GR: You know, I think originally it was one of the questions I had. How are we going to present this material in a way that does not offend anybody? Whether you see it in terms of Buddhism or

Christianity or any religion, I can understand when somebody has a religious bent and says, "I do not believe any of this." Maybe this material is coming out on the level of consciousness, but it also is coming out in on the level of heart, which a lot of Christians and other religious people understand. The material coming out shows both sides, and it shows a harmony in what a religious group would understand and what people strictly into consciousness would understand. They are like people sitting at different places in a room while watching one TV. They are seeing it through different angles, but they see the same thing.

S: Yeah. Right. What we are calling God is the pure energy field, and love is pouring out of it. The love going down this tube came out as Christianity to one and as Buddhism to another. There are lots of religious bents, but this love comes through each one. They are all coming from the same place. Maybe the First Principle is the only basic truth, and everything else is a truth because you believe it to be. So, this person believes in Christ, that person believes in Buddha, some other person believes in the Hindu Gods. This is like the blind men and the elephant. They all touch it but perceive something different.

GR: Right, and they are trying to figure out what they are touching.

S: What I get is the message that *we have all under-estimated God.*

GR: That is the challenge with this book. When you see an ordinary painting, it's just a two dimensional picture. But it's different when you see a painting that has life flowing through it. I almost cried in Italy when I saw a painting by Botticelli. It was like a hammer coming out and hitting me. It was incredible. He had the ability to put life in his painting, so I could experience what he was experiencing. I was so awed. I just stood there.

S: But out of ten people that see it, they are all going to have a different experience. They get what they are ready to get. You offer it, and they get what they get out of it.

GR: Yes.

S: So, I wonder, how you are you doing physically?

GR: I am doing okay. I still have some pain from time to time. I find I do not have any great joy in eating anymore because eating is associated with pain all the time. I am always asking myself, if I eat this, what is going to happen? It's like getting iron once a week. Each time the response is different. Yesterday is the first time in years that I felt like I had the energy to do something around the house. Maybe I was anemic for a long time and did not realize it. The weather wasn't too hot. It wasn't too cold. Everything seemed to be right. I did little projects here and there, and then I took a little breather, did another project, did some laundry, did the dishes, and did some organizing. In the evening I thought, "Man this is a red letter day. I have not done this in years." I am feeling a lot better.

S: That's good.

GR: One thing still leaves me feeling disappointed after all these years. I used to have lots of friends, and we were very active. We never sat down anywhere for very long. We were always up doing things. In Washington, there were a lot of beautiful places to visit. There are special little towns, and special little gifts that they make. One town does pies for some reason. Another town grows a lot of fruits, so they have fruit festivals all the time. When I left Washington and went to Colorado, Daren and I did some of that. I always had friends who liked to do that. After a while I had less and less energy. By the time I came back to Kauai, I did not even want to move. I wanted to stay still and relax and get a lot of sleep. Now I walk around for 15 minutes, and that's all I can do.

S: I know that one, given my thyroid problems all my life, but I find the more I am engaged in life, the less that becomes a big issue.

GR: Yeah. There is a part of me, though, that still wants to be out there. It's the explorer aspect of me. My basic goal was not to be famous or wealthy. My basic instinct was to observe. My motto was, "Those who stand and observe also serve." Then I got a little upset with myself because I didn't even have the energy to do that.

S: You've moved into a different phase now because of this work. You are getting unique information that needs to get out there.

GR: But at the same time the Guides say that I have to go out there into groups.

S: But you need the energy to do it.

GR: Exactly.

S: Well, maybe that is coming. It's finding its level. So, when is your surgery?

GR: It's April 8th. When I am in the hospital, I play opossum. I just sit there. I say, "Do whatever you have to do with me. I am not going to move. I am not going to do anything."

S: After the surgery, how long do they say you'll stay there?

GR: The surgeon said I will need at least seven days in the hospital.

S: That would be until the 15th, a full moon.

GR: That's interesting. The energy of the full moon.

S: It was so bright last night I thought it was the full moon, but it's actually tonight, or somewhere in there.

S: So, we have three more Sundays before the surgery to get together.

Okay. Well, let's see what the Guides says for us today.

We took a short break here. Grapo made himself comfortable on the sofa. He skipped all the preliminaries and went directly to a new scene where he found himself talking to a big egg.

Session 7 : The journey of Travelers

S: Okay. You say there is an egg. What color is the egg? Does it have a color?

GR: It's a big white egg about six feet tall.

S: That's a very big egg. Where are you in relationship to this egg?

GR: It looks like a farm of some kind.

S: Are there other animals at this place, on the farm, or is it the land?

GR: It's the land.

S: Is there anyone else there?

GR: I do not see anyone

S: Let's find out about you. I want you to take a look at your feet. Tell me about your feet.

GR: I'm barefooted.

S: Barefooted. From the look of your feet, can you say whether you are a young person or an older person?

GR: About middle age.

S: And do you feel that you are male or female?

GR: Male.

S: Does your body feel healthy?

GR: Yeah.

S: Are you wearing anything on your body?

GR: Pants, shirt.

S: Are there any ornaments on your body?

GR: No.

S: Are you carrying anything?

GR: No.

S: So, you are here in a male body, middle aged, barefooted, but wearing pants and shirt, not carrying anything or wearing any ornaments. And you are here with a big white egg.

GR: I am examining the egg. There does not seem to be anything unusual about it.

S: Except that it's big?

GR: Yes.

S: Let's find out why this egg is there. You can either speak to the egg itself, or you can ask and find out what information comes to you.

GR: I ask the egg why it's here. Why it's so big. The egg says "big" is relative.

S: That is a smarty answer. Relative seems in comparison to you, so that is important. Now we know the egg can give you answers. What would you like to ask the egg?

GR: The egg says that it's symbolic of the force of life, birthed into this world symbolically as a new egg, so we do not bring with us our perceived perceptions of other realities. We do not know where we come from or where we have been, so we can experience this world as it is. We can see this world with truly fresh eyes, with a degree of innocence. The shell is also symbolic of our protection as we come into this world. White is the symbol of purity.

GR: Why we don't come in with angels' wings instead of a white egg?

G: Not all Beings are angels. You are not an angel.

GR: How are we going to explain to mankind that the symbol of our purity and innocence coming into this world is a big white egg?

G: there is a yoke in it, like *joke*. Think of it more as a capsule than an egg.

GR: Why do we need a capsule to come into this world?

G: The journey can be treacherous. There are many worlds, and many Beings that travel to those worlds. All of them have their protection because the process can be treacherous. We are protected when we come into these worlds.

GR: Are there reptilians out there willing to eat us?

G: There are many energy forms. We do not want these energy forms to interfere with the process, so we are protected when we enter.

GR: Where do we come from?

G: You come from a light and energy world and travel through a vibration of energy, like a beam of light.

GR: I see an image of vibrating energy, violet in color, beaming into this world. I ask him if everybody comes this way.

G: No, there are many ways.

GR: It's how I came into this world from my original source world. I see a vision of my own home world. It's like a brilliant sun.

GR: What is my home world like? Is it a brilliant sun?

G: Gather into me the burning light.

GR: Why do we have to come here?

G: In furtherance of the work of the burning light. This light world is where all our brothers and sisters have gathered. We *see* you as shining light traveling to different worlds. The egg is symbolic of the protection in the process, so we are not interfered with. There are no reptilians that can gobble you up, and no other beings can interfere either. We are not touched with the light and the thought of the earth. We come into this world pure and untainted. The energies of other beings cannot interfere with our existence.

G: We do not come to this world to interfere. We come into this world to share our energy. We radiate this energy like magnets radiate their presence. That is our task. Yes, there are others who come to this world who have a different purpose. They serve in different ways. We know who they are. They serve in their way. We serve in ours. Our presence includes the physical world, the *Gaia*, and through the physical earth those energies help the other physical beings. This is your process and this is our process. We do not directly interfere with the energies of other beings, including the living earth, but we do have an influence. Yes, there are places in this world that have specific energy uses, energy spots, as they are called, but we do not use these.

G: We influence the totality of this world, not just one part. We know there are others using the portals of energy from this world, borrowing our energies, which encompass the totality of this world. There are cultures that use physical locations as a form of manifesting spiritual energy. We manifest the totality of this world, not one part or one place. This is my journey, this is your journey.

G: We do not need *a text* (as in scripture). We do not need written material. We share our energy with this world, and we seek knowledge and experience in this world. We do this automatically by being here. This process also helps to keep our world of Living Light in its pure form. That is why we are called Travelers. Our Living Light world is engaged with the living stream and the Source of Creation, the Source of Life. We exist hand in hand with the stream of life. There are others who come to this world who are transformed by the experience. We remain the same. We are pure light.

G: There are other beings who travel by ships, by manipulating themselves. Other beings take their physical form to this world. We do not do so. This transition for us is another point of travel. We can manipulate our bodies to travel through different worlds on different levels of consciousness, but our total Being does not change. We are immortal. Only the Living Light, the Source of Creation, can change what we are, can touch what we are. This is God's gift of immortality to us. We come to set the vibration of this world, the harmony of this world, and all other beings through the earth.

GR: Are all the worlds in this universe worlds of burning light, which do not burn the soul?

G: No, not all worlds are of the burning light, but we have been to many such worlds, and we do the same for them. The sound of the trumpet blows, and we obey. We are not angels, but we do come from the heart of creation, and through consciousness, we evolve. Our purpose is steady and on task, it's our dharma. We revel in joy at this process. We know no boundaries. We are aware of the living God, the living presence, but we are not one. We are separate but we walk hand in hand.

G: You understand the Gem Worlds of burning light that will ascend. We are of that world. When it's our time, our world of ever-burning light will ascend. Each species has their own method, their own process, and their own pace. They work for this purpose, some with greater clarity, others with less clarity. Our path is clear, unshakable, and unmovable. We exist in the plane that is eternal until it's our time to ascend. I am whole but also a particle of that world.

G: Many others you know have their own path, their own journey, and you will meet up with them from time to time, but you have your own purpose. You stand on this world, blazing light and energy, like magnetic waves, you share unto the earth, and it shares with all. The stream of life is part of all our journeys. It is our purpose to comprehend and to discern the process of creation. Not all of this world has the same purpose. But you will share your energies, your fields of magnetic waves, with all. That contact will not change you. You are steady and unchanging in this world. You cannot be manipulated, no matter how hard other beings will try. You need not fear them. They are shadows compared to your energy. They do not want to be in your presence, and they cannot do anything about it. You are like the rock, like the mountains in this world. From their perspective, you are immovable and unchanging, resolute. Be at peace.

S: Thank you so much for that message. That is very important. The imagery is very beautiful. The symbolism is perfect for that message you gave us today. Thank you. Now, I'd like to call Grapo's subconscious. We allow that being that spoke with us, to recede into its proper place, and as we thank it again, profoundly, for its message today. May I speak to Grapo's subconscious now?

GHS: Yes.

S: Thank you. I am very grateful to have the opportunity to meet with you again today. Grapo is doing a great job. It is been a pleasure to be with him almost every week and watch him change, watch him thrive, as though he's been given a new life that fulfills his ultimate purpose. As you know, we are engaged in bringing to the world the material that the Guides are giving us, so that other people can benefit from this perspective. Can you give us any help in how we can go about getting this material into the public realm?

GHS: The process is already in place. We do not see the results yet.

S: So, we are being guided?

GHS: Yes. It is unfolding.

S: Okay. I'd also like to ask about the physical changes for Grapo with this project going on. It would be really lovely if he could have more energy, feel better in his body, and have a successful surgery. That feels to me like he is getting a step up. Am I correct in that feeling?

GHS: He's in the process of allowing us to help him. That is why he has an attitude of *lay back and let it happen*.

S: And he need not be active in that process.

GHS: There are others there who are assisting him in this process.

S: Does he need to do anything in particular himself?

GHS: No.

S: Very good, thank you. I am going to ask, finally, if you can connect with my own subconscious, and let me know something about my physical stamina to keep up with this project. Would you please comment on that?

GHS: Yes. You are assisted. All that is necessary for you to do is put your attention on the project. The process is an automatic one. You both are in good hands.

S: Well, that makes my heart sing. Thank you.

GHS: Be at peace.

S: So, are we complete for today?

GHS: Yes.

S: Thank you.

CHAPTER 9

FINDING OUR WAY HOME

Session 8: Sister and the Cave

Grapo arrives in an open field carpeted in wild flowers. There is a slight breeze, a clear sky, sunny and temperate. It's the middle of the day. In an instant he is standing in a cave. Sister is there waiting for him.

GHS: I wonder if this world has a name. I ask Sister why we are in this cave. She says it's as good as any other cave.

S: Welcome, Sister. We are glad to be with you today. What is it that you want to tell us today?

GHS: She's thinking about it. She says I come with many questions. This is a good place because there are no attachments to it.

S: Are you looking out of the cave into the landscape or looking into the cave?

GHS: I am looking inside. There seems to be a fire, a crystal-like fire, and a light is coming out of it. I ask if we have done this before. She says many times.

S: Do you do this consistently with Grapo in this dimension, like in his night work, or are you talking in a bigger perspective?

GHS: She says this is our favorite place, away from everybody, so we can focus on one another.

S: Well, Sister, would you like to begin a conversation, or are you aware of his questions?

GHS: I think she's waiting for me to ask the right question.

S: Uh huh. So, has a right question come to you yet?

GHS: She says a shell is not as simple as it seems to be. It's complex, like a matrix, and that's how the universe is — very complex, very structured. She says our place in the universe is not random, yet it's not specific. It's not predetermined, but it has a purpose. I ask her why there are so many different understandings of what we perceive as reality. She says that it's due to each individual's particular frequency, which allows individuals to see what they need to see. She says that from the human perspective, the view is limited. The view is not contingent on consciousness, but on each individual's frequency.

GHS: I am asking her, "How do we see the whole picture rather than through our specific frequency?" She says it's done through consciousness. Through consciousness, we can leave behind a particular frequency of the personality to see the whole picture, a clearer picture. The cave is a metaphor for leaving behind the frequencies. We come here to leave behind our frequency and open our consciousness to the whole picture. The crystal fire is a metaphor for our pureness, our core being, and a light that shines through us. I ask her about the Home world. She said it's far beyond this galaxy.

S: Was this Grapo's home world, or is it the bigger home world?

GHS: No, she's speaking in terms of my home world.

S: Okay.

GHS: I ask why is it that I do not feel the emotions of the home world. She says it's because of the distance, but my brothers and sisters are shining their light upon me. I ask her what is the relationship between the physical world, the Burning Worlds, and our home world. She says, in terms of distance, it's beyond comprehension. Many, many light years.

She says there are many worlds that are preparing for their final ascension, which we are working hard to prepare. She says the time is near, as far as I can understand what time is. There may be brothers and sisters in different worlds assisting.

GHS: I ask her why there seems to be a difference between spirituality and the physical world. We seem to think they are two different things. She says, "The physical world is also God, or God's structure. There are physical worlds that you can visit in a physical body. There are spiritual worlds you can visit in a spiritual sense. The complexity of this causes confusion for the human perspective.

GHS: I asked her how this world can understand or have clarity. She says it's through the flight of the dove, through peace, not peace with others, but peace **within** the individual. The crystal light is the physical aspect, and the flight of the peace dove is the spiritual aspect. Both worlds coexist simultaneously. They are not side-by-side.

GHS: I ask her, what is the difference between helping each individual versus my task of assisting the entire planet physically and then assisting through the planet? She says they are different things, and there are many different possibilities. By helping through the planet, bringing the energy through the planet, this helps every individual in his or her own way. She says there are many people, like messiahs and others, who came to earth to share their visions of spirituality. Their visions are tempered by the physical world, the energies of this world. So, while there are some who come to help in a spiritual sense, some come to help in a physical sense by enlivening the spiritual well being of this planet. There are those who walk on water, and there are those who walk on beams of light, each serving their purpose.

GHS: I ask if there is a difference between the spiritual beings that come to earth as pillars of light. She says there are many who come. You perceive them in ships. Although they have that aspect of spirituality and light, they are different. Take this in the context of their own expression of light and spirit. There are many beings in this world who seek their assistance, who look for their help as part of their process. We are not one of them.

GHS: I ask if humanity will ever resolve their multiple visions into one singularity or understanding. She says, yes, the same as we have done in the Gem Worlds. Some day we will achieve that.

GHS: I ask how the First Principle will assist them. She says it will provide a path of clarity, in the spiritual sense and in the physical sense. She says that even the other beings you seek, who use their ships, would like to visit the Gem Worlds, but it's not possible for them at this time. She says, "There are many people on this planet seeking understanding of their role, their path. The light that we bring to this planet helps them achieve that." As we support the Gaia Being, the planet supports the individual.

GHS: I ask why there are so many different levels of understanding, so many different kinds of records being kept. She says, "There are many levels of spiritual development where knowledge is being maintained. Our knowledge is maintained in our very Being in the light worlds. Our knowledge is part of our very Being of Light. There are others who keep records, who seek knowledge through that information. The knowledge we bring out is meant to help apply clarity to show that each individual has a path. The paths may not be the same. Mankind need not find a resolution to all of their different beliefs, their need to know that causes them to seek and find paths, to seek resolution in the physical world. We only maintain your presence here. It is through your light path that you ascend, that you evolve, that you comprehend. Resolution is not the solution. That is why you bring forth The First Principle. It is like an arrow flying through the air, giving you direction, and will help bring clarity. And there are teachings, philosophies, which seeks to transcend religion, which seeks to know the light path."

GHS: I ask her if there is anything else we should know. She says there are many dark worlds that are beginning their process. I ask how we can help these dark worlds. She says there is not much we can do. This world is not one of them. "We help those that we can help," she says.

She's now asking if you have any specific questions.

S: Oh, thank you, Sister. I wasn't expecting that. We are attempting to help other people on this planet by putting out a book with the information you and the Guides are giving us. Earlier we were talking about having a concluding session. Is this appropriate?

GHS: Yes, and there are many conclusions. This is not one of them.

S: Okay. Thank you. Well, let me ask, was it you also who showed up as the cowboy, or was that a different Guide?

GHS: There are many different Guides.

S: Different Guides, okay.

GHS: I assist because he [Grapo] is part of our world.

S: Uh-huh.

GHS: Continue if you have any other questions.

S: Okay. I am asking my Guidance to inform me if there are other things I need to ask. Give me a moment here. From what you can see of how we are approaching getting out this material, are we on the right track, or the most appropriate track?

GHS: Yes.

S: Thank you. We are very grateful for that. It makes it much easier for us. We are on track in looking for help to get this book published. Is that correct?

GHS: Yes, and please understand that Life is Guidance.

S: Okay. It seems that was another question we had. Does Grapo's home world have a name?

GHS: Yes. It does have a name.

S: What is the name of Grapo's home world?

GHS: It's difficult to pronounce.

S: Can you spell it?

GHS: No. It sounds like Heliocyte, Helio...

S: Is it Helios?

GHS: Something like that. It does not have a pronunciation in your worlds.

S: The Helios that I know, that I have contacted, is from the sun.

GHS: Yes His home world is a *Burning World.* The name that the people of my home world call it cannot be pronounced here. It is outside the range of your language.

S: Well, you've showed Grapo a picture of it, and he certainly has a feeling about it. Thank you for that. Would there be a symbol that could represent his home world?

GHS: His home world is part of the matrix of Gem Worlds, of other Beings. A symbol of the Gem Worlds is pure light. Gem Worlds exist at the very cusp of Creation.

S: Can you give us, in our language, a statement that would be a guiding sentence for the book that we are going to be doing here? Does that make sense?

GHS: The First Principle is self-explanatory. Anything I would say specifically would only cause greater confusion.

S: Okay. Well, would it be appropriate, then, for us to emphasize the First Principle right from the beginning, and then restate it as it keeps coming up, so that it's integrated for the reader?

GHS: This is for you to decide.

S: Okay. Well, we'll do the best we can with it.

GHS: Be at peace.

S: Thank you so much for coming again to be with us.

Here we ended the session and continued our discussion of what happened.

GR: I am thinking about the knowledge coming through and the level of contact we are making. When she talked about the Gem Worlds, that they exist at the cusp of Creation, I was able to look down from the Gem Worlds, and it was incredible. It is like black ink going down into this physical reality. That is amazing. How would anybody make a decision to go down there?

S: Really...

GR: And she seemed to think it was important to understand the point she was making about the egg and the shell, that because Creation is so varied, so complex, that there are so many individuals saying so many different things, experiencing different understandings.

We tend to see everything from this perspective of wanting to see the light, and playfulness, and peace, and all this. But she also pointed out that part of the Creation is darkness, I mean, really primitive black places. I was asking how could we help them and she said, "You cannot help them. You can only help those who are ready for it." She said our world, is not one of those dark black places. In fact, she kept giving me the image that the light coming to this world has already passed over it, and we're now in the process of, for lack of a better word, enlightenment. It's no longer a possibility, it's a reality. At some points in time, like in the darkest places, it's not a possibility.

I kept asking about this path and that path. She says there are two paths, but only one path in the sense that we do both at the same time. One is a spiritual path, wherein messiahs like the Christ come to earth to help us *see.* And there is also a physical path, which we are helping by bringing the light and sharing it with a physical world, like the earth. As the light of the earth becomes stronger in the physical sense, then the individuals on the planet become more evolved. So, there are two things going on at the same time. One in the spiritual sense and one in the physical sense. The physical sense comes through a spiritual light, and that is a Gem Worlds kind of thing.

We come as physical beings of light that manifest into this world so we can share our light with the earth and help mankind. We are not specifically going to any particular group to help them. And she said there are beings that we see, like UFO's, who are enlightened and lighter beings, maybe not of pure light, who are being asked to help. Their presence is becoming known because people on earth are asking them for help. There are some who ask for the messiah, there are some who ask for physical beings. Both are helping. One is not against the other. Both are part of the same process. That is where they need to be for their own purpose or their own evolution.

I kept asking, "How can we help everybody?"

She says, "You are helping everyone indirectly. You cannot specifically help each individual. That is their path and that is their knowingness. That is their light. They help themselves." That is why she said what she said: Life is Guidance.

Life is Guidance because everything in life is about Guidance, whether on an individual level or a group level, or an entire galaxy level. Life is Guidance. She got a little confused because you were asking her for a conclusion for the book. In her perspective, there is only one conclusion, and that is the final ascension of the Gem Worlds. For us, it's not about a totally final conclusion. It's about parts of conclusions -- because we do not see what is going on in a holistic way. We see in a partial way. So, as far as writing the book, she says the best way to do it is what came across anyway, what we think provides the greatest clarity, because we are not writing it for them. They do not need it. We are writing it for the rest of humanity.

S: Yes.

GR: I got a little frustrated in the process because it felt so open ended in some sense. I kept asking for specifics, and she kept throwing me greater wholeness.

S: Right, yeah.

GR: So, she provided a lot more clarity, but we are still trying to get specifics in the system of Creation that is extremely complex. She cannot bring it down even to our level of understanding because we are not anywhere close. It's that translation between talking with a light being and talking to my sisters versus my consciousness here now trying to comprehend the wholeness. It's restrictive because my purpose here is a different one than some other people's purpose. There are lots of people in this world who come to help people on an individual basis, and they go into religion or they go into philosophies. My perspective is a little bit different from theirs.

S: Can you tell me what is your perspective?

GR: I desire to help people here, but it's not my purpose. My purpose is to come here and be a light anchor for the earth and transmit the energies to the earth itself. This is an indirect way of helping mankind. Sure, there is a sense of me as an individual that says it would be great if I could help other people. From my perspective as one who is given the knowledge, who is bringing the knowledge, bringing some value of clarity to the knowledge, I am helping people on an individual basis. That is why she's giving out all this knowledge, to help on that level, but that is not my purpose.

S: Well, it's kind of a branch of your tree?

GR: Yeah. Basically, I mean, if you want to help, you might as well help in the most holistic way you can, because then a lot of different levels get touched.

S: By being a light anchor. That is the biggest part of it. Because we are human, and we are living this life, we see the ways people get initiated or get inspired, so we are doing that aspect of it with this work together.

GR: Yeah.

S: I know. I am a light energy worker, too, and we have talked about this before, about going into a shop or something, and all of a sudden a bunch of people show up.

GR: Yeah. This is one of the things she clued me in on. I was asking her something about the world. She says there are other light worlds, not Gem Worlds, but other light worlds that come here, too. It's like a whole group.

S: Yeah. It's very complex.

GR: That is why she says there is confusion and doubt on this planet. Everybody is giving out their own little story, and people are thinking, "Well, maybe that is my path, too." That is what I'm doing, in a way. She says everybody has their own path, a unique path, and a unique purpose. What the Guides are trying to do with the First Principle, bringing out the First Principle is showing some level of wholeness about these paths.

S: That's good.

GR: She's trying to provide a framework from which everybody can understand what is going on. And that's not to say, your path is right, and someone else's path is not right.

S: That is the problem we have throughout history.

GR: She's saying the real issue is that we each have a means to our evolution. It may not seem like the fastest means, but it's the means each individual can understand.

S: Yes.

GR: That is part of the reason why there is confusion. People are trying to see their path through somebody else's path. What the Guides are trying to bring out in the First Principle is the need to see the whole picture, that as an individual you find your path through seeing that wholeness. That is why they say to stop trying to find resolution.

Resolution is not the answer, nor, is showing the whole picture. Doing your path in your particular way is the solution.

S: Well, she did say that you are not the solution, but that is the way it is. Each person has to do his or her own path.

GR: Part of the First Principle is that no matter what path you choose, whether you are on a shamanic or religious path, whatever path you choose, all of it is a guise of Creation. It's all part of Creation. That is why they say Life is Guidance. She basically told me to stop trying to mettle. I meddle in the sense that I am trying to find solutions to things that are not part of my purpose.

CHAPTER 10
OUR NEW BURNING WORLD

Session 9: The Final Session

*A*s Grapo and I move into the final session, we hope for some kind of spectacular finale. Guidance gives us what we get. This session starts as usual. Grapo moves into the Theta state and begins to breath deeply, as he always does once the Guides have connected with him.

For awhile now in working together, both of us are permitted to ask questions. Sometimes the Guide gives us a longer dialogue when no questions are being asked.

The setting this time is a beach. Grapo sees and then enters an empty garage that seems to be a place where boats would be kept. There is a male figure waiting there for him. Grapo and the Guide both seem to be about middle aged and are dressed similarly in boots with no laces, brown pants, a white shirt, and some sort of a vest.

Grapo's first question begins the conversation.

GR: Why are we in a garage space?

G: This place is a metaphor for getting ready to leave. The journey is only beginning. We have been journeying together for many lifetimes.

GR: This is a new Guide that I have not met before.

G: We have journeyed together before and will do so again. We come from the stars, but we always end up on a rock. Now we are doing one final journey in this physical world. It's not like any we have done before. The journey is going to be unique for a lot of people on this planet. Lots of people have wishes and desires about what is to come next, but Dharma is always upheld.

S: What is this Dharma?

G: The basic principles of the cosmos or individual existence must be fulfilled. It's our journey. The universe is full of light. The light is getting brighter. You can see it all around us. This means greater clarity for people because existence in the new world means to be in a brighter light vibration. There is greater light on the earth now. This is more like the new world to which you are journeying.

There is a journey for mankind and a journey for the planet. These are different journeys. There is greater light, freedom and clarity in the next world. There is physical form in the new world, but not as many boundaries. It is like seeing and feeling in a different way.

GR: Is this heaven?

G : Heaven stands beside us, but this is not heaven. In this new world people will not be working in the darkness but will be in the light. People will be able to travel, not around the world, but can travel throughout the Universe.

GR: Will all of humanity be doing this?

G: All of humanity will be doing this, but not at this time. They are a little behind in their timing. Most of humanity still needs solid boundaries -- rocks and trees and grounds. In this new world, you can see in infinite directions. There are no boundaries. There are structures. You cannot see them from here because you need to be tuned to a higher vibration.

We in the new world are not bound by planets. We can travel these places. We have a human form, but it's much lighter. We have much more energy. As you now travel from city to city, we travel across the Universe.

GR: How does this express the First Principle?

G: Here there are no brakes to stop us from the leap. There are no boundaries. We are not bound by the weather or any other boundaries. Humanity has a "solid" concept of what reality is like. Eventually, they will move out of that reality and be free.

GR: What part does consciousness play in the new world?

G: We are still bound by consciousness, but there are many here who can raise their consciousness if they choose. We are free of daily requirements, such as the production of food. These boundaries no longer apply. This is a place of a higher vibration of the First Principle. Mankind is moving in this direction.

GR: I see before me fields of light going on forever, layer upon layer. There are no stars here.

G: Planets are bound by their physical size or shape. Here they are more like membranes of light. Each layer has characteristics of expression. Earth has its own expression. We here in the new world are freer. Here boundaries are not as strong. There are other concepts in humanity's understanding that will have to melt away.

We still journey here as we do on earth, from place to place. There is much to explore in this place. It has many layers. This is a higher expression of the First Principle. You can travel to golden cities if you wish, but it's not the end or the beginning. There is much more to experience.

GR: How is this new world related to heaven?

G: Heaven is a reflection of this existence. Heaven is a temporary place for rejuvenation.

GR: I am trying to see what is beyond the place where I am standing. I cannot. This is a new world, a new experience even for me. I can feel my brothers and sisters in the home world cheering. They are happy that I am out of the muck of the physical world.

I ask the Guide, "Will the rest of humanity join me?"

He says, "In time, yes. The First Principle applies. They are moving forward although they are not quite here yet."

GR: Will the earth split into two worlds?

G: This is a metaphor. Humanity will not all make it all at once. Each level of movement has it's own level of consciousness; it's own level of reality. Earth has its level of consciousness. The next world is a plane of light rather than a physical world. This level of existence is beyond most of humanity's understanding at this time.

GR: I still see a physical body, but it's different. I see a different body, partly made of light. There is no concept of distance or direction.

G: There are many steps that humanity will take to reach this place. Even now it's beyond their concept. Physics in consciousness is transformed here. Physics still applies, but it's viewed from a different perspective. In your world, you have to travel in a car. In this world, travel is mainly by desire. Both consciousness and physics work together. It's a spontaneous reaction.

GR: I am trying to see this world. I have difficulty seeing. It's a light, but not the same as my home world. It's a lesser quality light than home, but more than the present earth. I am too new to see the structures here.

G: The five senses have to be tuned differently. That is why you are having difficulty seeing it. You do not have that tuning yet. The UFOs are on the lower levels of this dimensionality. They exist on the lower membranes of light. Here we see worlds as membranes upon membranes of light.

GR: How do the streams of light relate to this new world?

G: It flattens out here. It expands into the membranes. In this reality, there is less differentiating between streams of light and the membranes of light. It still streams to the Source.

GR: How would humanity feel emotionally in response to this place, if it were here now?

G: They would feel the particles of light flowing and churning. Yes, there are emotions here, too, but they are physically expressed differently here. They cannot perceive of this world because it's too alien to their minds, alien to their consciousness. You still feel a sense of being an individual here although at the same time there is incredible infinity in all directions.

GR: Why did you bring me here?

G: This is your individual self-journey. This is your path. For others, it's not the right time. This place is the final expression of the First Principle in which humanity is heading.

Be At Peace

We end the transcribed transmissions here. There is no end to the Being of the soul. It will travel and re-express itself infinitely, it seems. There are things we cannot see from here.

The Guides have given us a different way to look and experience who we are, what we are doing here and beyond. The Guides have given us messages to spark a new understanding of reality and the possibilities inherent in The First Principle.

There is a lot to integrate.

Grapo and I are pleased that we could share this with you, and we hope you will find the Peace that the Guides invoke at the end of each session. That is their wish and their offering to you.

Be At Peace.

STATEMENT FROM SUZANNE

I have been working with the material transmitted through Grapo for nine months, as I write this. The implications are still unfolding for me. In this section I have written up my personal insights and speculations on the meanings of these transmissions. Perhaps this will help you notice how these messages are creating changes in your own reality.

Most of us see the field of All That Is in a linear fashion. That is what we do here in this world. That linear view must be expanded to a perception of multi-levels, all interacting, existing simultaneously, affecting us all as everything moves and expands according to the First Principle. Additionally, we are being asked to see all of Creation as a tiny speck in the field of All That Is.

I speculate that we are not traveling in a linear sense when we talk of going Home to Source. When we let go of all attachments, and move out of Creation, we move into the field of All That Is. At that point we are Home. There is no need in that place to go anywhere or be anything. We exist as the eternal presence.

There are things, we were told, that we would not understand from here in this reality. Creation has much more to be explored in it. We are gluttons for experiences, so we are likely to continue to the next Burning World to explore more and continue further in the movement of The First Principle.

From working with Grapo's information from the Guides, these are the ten qualities that I have experienced and anchored in myself.

1. A *greater understanding* of the process of humanity's journey back Home, back to Source.
2. A *peacefulness* in my soul concerning the supposed dilemma of humanity's search for itself.
3. A *settled knowing* that Home exists, and I am destined to return there. The longing is at rest because I know this is the truth.
4. A *steady appreciation* of Creation in all its forms. Even the "bad" things. Everything is as it is.
5. *An acceptance* of being human. This acceptance finds me at peace with this aspect of the total journey out from Home and back again.
6. *Patience* for the unfolding. There is no rush. I can stop and smell the flowers with no concern that I am wasting time.
7. A *greater connection* with Guidance entities as well as my own higher self.
8. *Release of the attachment* to things, i.e., cars, houses, food, clothes, memorabilia. I can have and enjoy them without attachment or judgment. They are part of the creation I am in, but they are not mine.
9. *Respect* for each individual's journey. Each is different, and each is precious.
10. *Love growing less and less conditional in every moment.*

That all sounds quite perfect, and yet, there is still some anger and fear in me. I still abuse my self with my thoughts. Yet I know these are choices I am making. I can choose otherwise. It's all in a days work.

I hope you have enjoyed the journey revealed here. Play with it. Find what fits for you and what does not. Maybe there will be more later. I have been profoundly affected by it, and my gratitude supports me in seeing that this gets published and made available for you.

If you are an explorer of consciousness, I highly recommend that you find a Quantum Healing Hypnosis Therapy (QHHT) practitioner in your area. It's the easiest and fastest way to get to your own Higher Self and Guidance where all your unique answers to everything can be found.

To find a practitioner, please go to www.dolorescannon.com. We live and work all over the world. We are individually and collectively dedicated to your greater connection with a reality that brings you the most fulfilling life possible.

Blessings,
Suzanne

STATEMENT FROM GRAPO

I was in a QHHT session here on Kauai. QHHT is the Quantum Healing Hypnosis Therapy taught by Dolores Cannon. If you have not heard about it, you can look into it.

I went for a session with Suzanne Franzen and I came out of that session with a conscious connection with Source. My own subconscious spoke and so did my Guide. Other Guides showed up as we went along with more sessions. The story unfolded in unexpected ways. We were told that this material would be a book. It would contain new information on the evolution of man and of the planet. Astonishingly, they also introduced us to the next steps for humanity. We are on an amazing journey.

For me, the greatest thing about this was the energy from being in the presence of the Guides. It's the most profound experience of my life. I have spent years meditating, and this QHHT stuff got me there in a flash. Like a snap of the fingers, I suddenly was in the stream, outside of Creation, traveling Home. I saw all of Creation as only a tiny speck in All That Is. I was taken on journeys that revealed how we put on the brakes in our journey to Source, and what we do to keep ourselves stuck in reincarnating. It was also shown to me, how we can get on with our return journey to Home.

Grapo

GLOSSARY

All that Is: The infinitude of existence in all dimensions in all universes.

Burning Worlds: We see them as blue and green, but their essence is the fire, the gift of Source, which is *love*. We have been concerned with saving the earth. This is the big game we are playing here. We are trying to change things in this world. Within this material, we are being shown that such a goal is impossible. While we are here on earth, it's our best option to play with all that is available. In this view of the evolution of many earths, we see that this world of ours will continue to be a world of limitation and separation. When a soul is ready, it advances to the next Burning World. There are many of these worlds. They are not all in this dimension, but they all are in Creation. They are what we are wishing to find and what we know about on a deep level. We do not need to change this world; we, like Gaia, are responsible for our own evolution which will propel us towards what we are seeking in the next Burning World.

Creation: Our created universe is really, really, really huge, from our perspective. In the infinitude of Source, Creation is only a tiny speck. Creation is ever expanding and contains everything. All Gods, dimensions, parallel lives, galaxies, universes, the meta-verse, everything in form and not in form.

First Principle: The First Principle is absolute existence. In the beginning there was light. There was a physical creation and, simultaneously, an expansion of consciousness. As we evolve, we are not evolving on our own through physical expansion. The expansion of consciousness is driving us. It's the motivating force, the Living Light from the Source. We are striving to reach Source. It's an unstoppable flow, nothing stops it. You can apply brakes, slow down, experience this world and all of Creation, but you are constantly and always moving in the direction of expanding consciousness. The absolute reality is a stream of movement from the beginnings of Creation and back to the Source. That whole process of going from the Big Bang to Light, to Consciousness, to the Source. That is the First Principle. That is the most important thing within All That Is. It's the absolute thing that exists so absolutely that it can become invisible and be forgotten for the sake of experience. The First Principle means that there is an inescapable movement forward.

Following Your Path: Be reassured there are no wrong choices, simply choices made on different levels resulting in different effects and experiences. Following your path may lead to reincarnation on this planet. There are so many experiences to explore. It's ever expanding, and there will always be more to experience. We may go on to the next Burning World, or we may go beyond Creation back Home to Source.

Going Home: When we have completed our adventures in Creation, there is a desire to go Home and be in Source again. At this point, we must release all attachments to get out of Creation. This is the inevitable flow of our Being.

Putting On The Brakes: As conscious souls, something comes into our field of awareness. It's Creation. We are fascinated by that tiny speck in the infinitude of Source. We decide to investigate. We put on the brakes.

Source: The infinitude. All That Is. The fabric and intelligence from which All arise and to which All return.

Made in the USA
Middletown, DE
18 March 2016